From Pharaoh's Lips

From Pharaoh's Lips

Ancient Egyptian Language in the Arabic of Today

Ahmad Abdel-Hamid Youssef

Introduced by Fayza Haikal

Illustrations by Golo

The American University in Cairo Press

Cairo New York

113 Sharia Kasr el Aini, Cairo, Egypt
420 Fifth Avenue, New York, NY 10018
www.aucpress.com

Dar el Kutub No. 16732/01
ISBN 978 977 424 708 8

5 6 7 8 9 10 11 12 14 13

Designed by AWH / AUC Press Design Center
Printed in Egypt

Contents

Introduction
by Fayza Haikal

With the advent of Islam and its sweeping expansions in the world, Egypt was conquered by the Arabs in 641 and the course of its history changed radically. People gradually converted to Islam, and the upper strata of the population started to learn Arabic, as they had learned Greek before, in the Hellenistic period, because it was the language of the rulers and was gradually becoming the language of administration. Arabic was also the language of the Qur'an, but countries of the Muslim world that were not administered by Arabs did not find it necessary to learn their language. In Egypt, the shift to Islam was probably easier than the shift to a new language for, after all, when the country was conquered by the Arabs in the seventh century, most Egyptians were religious people, believing in God and in the Beyond, even when their respective religions were not as rigorously monotheistic as Islam. But even in the new religion, the shift was not radical. Traces of the 'old traditions' that did not touch upon the dogma of absolute monotheism are still present today, having been slowly reinterpreted, absorbed, and included in the cycle of the new religious festivities of the country. Such 'adaptations' are particularly evident in the realm of funerary practices and the mulids or festivals in memory of deceased religious personalities in Egypt.[1]

The shift from Coptic to Arabic was probably more gradual, particularly among Christians or in circles remote from the management and political administration of the country. For, as Michael Agar writes: "You can't use a new language unless you change the consciousness that is tied to the old one, unless you stretch beyond the circle of grammar and dictionary, out of the old world and into a new one."[2] And how could you abruptly change "the consciousness that is tied to the old one" if you keep living in the same place, with the same people and the same traditions and environment, even if you have new rulers and slightly altered religious creeds? Until the massive immigration of Arabs into the country in the early eighth century, when Arabic became the official language of administration, there was no real urge among the population to learn the rulers' language, and Arabic must have been initially acquired as a second language next to Coptic to be used only in specific walks of a person's life. It is difficult to tell why or when exactly Coptic died out as a spoken language, and it is very probable that this phenomenon varied according to the different strata of the population and to different geographical locations in the country. But it is interesting to note that as of the eleventh century, there are no more documents relating to daily life in Egypt still written in Coptic and that by the end of the twelfth century Arabic had become the main written language of the church, indicating that the population could no longer understand Coptic. Nevertheless, during the process of arabization, many words belonging to the old tongue remained in use, enriching the vocabulary of the new one and giving it its particular flavor. In the same way, expressions and metaphors drawn essentially from the environment and from social behavior were translated from Egyptian/Coptic into Arabic, because the way Egyptians viewed their world and expressed their age-old feelings and wisdom had not changed with the change of language. This is a common phenomenon across time and space. Often when you speak a number of languages you have a tendency to introduce words from one of them into the other because you think they express better what you want to convey. In scientific publications we still come across some Latin expressions or a German word that render, in a compact manner, what another language would say in many words. English technical words that were coined by Anglo-Saxons for their new inventions are now also used internationally. In a similar way, this is what happened to Egyptians who spoke Arabic but felt that a word of their old language expressed better what they wanted to convey or who, fearing that their interlocutor might not understand the equivalent Arabic word, repeated it in Coptic or created a composite of both.[3]

It seems that Coptic words were more persistently used in the countryside away from the big cosmopolitan agglomeration or the arabized centers of administration. They also remained in the technical jargon of traditional professions related to the land and to the Nile and in the vocabulary commonly used in the home. Needless to say, in order to detect such words in the modern vernacular one must have a good command of both Arabic and Coptic and be able to establish their etymologies, for not all loan words in Egyptian Arabic come from Coptic. In fact, our modern vernacular includes words from most of the languages of the nations that have invaded Egypt from the Persians to modern times and who stayed long enough in the country to have some impact on its people.

But a language includes more than just grammar and vocabulary. In order to really understand it, "to live in it, all those meanings that go beyond grammar and the dictionary have to fit somewhere."[4] As I noted above, there are expressions and metaphors that passed from Egyptian to Arabic, such as 'fat on honey,' to indicate harmony and good relations, which is one of the examples in this book. Sometimes, when these expressions reflect a reality common to most people, they pass unnoticed. But when they reflect the particular environment and experience of the people who created them, they can sometimes be very local. You have to live their culture to be able to appreciate them and they can be difficult for a foreign translator to apprehend.[5]

From Pharaoh's Lips is a charming story that condenses and illustrates a huge amount of research on the strength and persistence of culture in Egypt, in spite of the changes in language and religion that historical events have introduced in the country. I would like to thank the author for bringing home this important concept. Thanks are also due to Dr. Mary Knight for her professional compilation of the glossaries and to Golo for his enlivening illustrations.

Notes

1. Examples of such 'survivals' have been studied at length, firstly by foreign scholars, who were struck by analogies they noticed between modern behavior and the scenes of daily life that cover the walls of ancient tombs or by modern practices they compared with what they knew of ancient Egypt. Later on, Egyptian scholars started to observe their own culture and 'ethno-Egyptology' gradually became a common approach to ancient Egypt in our national universities, and much research is done on social behavior, folk medicine, funerary traditions, religious expressions, and so on, that link the past with the present and allow for a better understanding of both. See, for example, W. Blackman, *The Fellahin of Upper Egypt*, The American University in Cairo Press, 2000; N. Abu Zahra,

"Isis and al-Sayyida Zaynab: Links to Ancient Egypt" in W. Wendrich and G. van der Kooij, eds., *Moving Matters: Ethnoarchaeology in the Near East*, Research School of Asian, African, and Amerindian Studies, University of Leiden, 2002, 215–24; N. El-Shohoumi, "Burying the Dead—Vivifying the Past," in Wendrich and van der Kooij, 189–213; S-A. Naguib, "Miroirs du Passé," *Cahiers de la Societe d'Egyptologie*, vol. 2, Geneva, 1993; S. Sonbol and T. Atia, *Mulid! Carnivals of Faith*, The American University in Cairo Press, 1999; and many more.

2 M. Agar, *Language Shock: Understanding the Culture of Conversation*, New York: William Morrow, 1994, 22.

3 Lists of such words have often been compiled, firstly by Egyptian Copts and then by scholars of other denominations. Today this field of research attracts a number of young Egyptian researchers and I do hope that we shall soon have all the Coptic etymologies systematically added to dictionaries of colloquial Arabic.

4 Agar, *Language Shock*, 10.

5 The usage of such terms as 'water,' 'canal,' or 'river,' for example, as reference for comparisons or as metaphors for a number of other things is also typically Egyptian, today as in the past. See for example F. Haikal, "L'eau dans les metaphores de l'Egypte Ancienne" in B. Menu, ed., *Les problèmes institutionnels de l'eau en Egypte ancienne et dans l'antiquité mediterranéenne*, Cairo: Institut Français d'Archéologie Orientale, 1994.

1

The Past Remains Alive

"Lost is he who deserts his past!"

من فات قديمه تاه

mīn fāt qadīmuh tāh

This proverb is heard throughout Egypt from south to north. For most Egyptians, the past has never left us. Our remote history and old traditions still occupy a large place in our culture and everyday life, although we are often unaware of this continuity. The above proverb echoes an even older one spoken by our ancestors thousands of years ago:

"Any knowledgeable person is one who will listen to what the ancestors said"

(Urk IV 1984, ZÄS 60, 75)

rḫw-ḫt pw nb sḏm.ty.fy ḏdt.n tpjw-ʿ ỉmyw-ḥꜣt

This little book is about what our ancestors said—and what we still say. Some words and expressions are practically unchanged from the time of the earliest pharaohs. Others continue in use with slight changes in pronunciation or meaning. "Egypt is the mother of the world" مصر ام الدنيا *Maṣr umm al-dunya* is one of the very old proverbs heard down to the present day. It gives the Egyptians the feeling of noble descent and inherited wisdom. Hence, though sometimes eclipsed by some intrusive adoptions, came the unbroken chain of tradition together with an enormous number of ancient Egyptian words and idioms still currently used, especially in the countryside.

The ancient Egyptian language is one of the oldest languages on earth to be written. Hieroglyphs are 'pictures' that represent *sounds* of that ancient language or *ideas*. So, for example, the word *st* (probably pronounced *sit* or *set*), which means 'woman,' was written with hieroglyphic signs for the sounds *s* and *t*, which were followed by a determinative that represented the idea, or category, of the person or thing named:

You will note that the vowels are not usually written in Egyptian—as in modern Arabic:

ستّ *sitt*

Moreover, some hieroglyphs represent more than one consonantal sound, such as the 𓉐, *pr,* in 𓉐𓉻, *pr ꜥꜣ*, meaning 'pharaoh.' The number of signs grew over time from about seven hundred in the Old Kingdom to several thousand in the Roman period, although there was a trend toward using signs for their phonetic value even more than for their pictographic value. The 'alphabet' is still used by modern Egyptians, especially for writing the names of Egyptians and foreigners in gold or silver cartouche pendants sold as souvenirs. (The cartouche is normally an oval in which royal names were written. It was often drawn as a pair of twisted ropes, tied at one end, that encircles the hieroglyphs of the name, most probably as a visual way of saying that the pharaoh was the ruler of everything encircled by the sun.) For example, we find the name Ramesses on ancient monuments:

 *Rꜥ-ms-sw*

or we can write our own using the hieroglyphic alphabet:

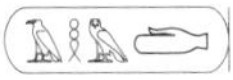 *ꜣḥmd,* 'Ahmad'

Over time, because hieroglyphs were ideally suited for stone and not for pen and papyrus, two new varieties of writing developed based directly on the hieroglyphs. These are called hieratic ('religious' or 'priestly' script) and Demotic ('the people's' script).

When the Greeks arrived with Alexander the Great in 331 BC, they brought with them the Greek alphabet and language, which were then used for most official business. The native Egyptian writing continued, however. Cleopatra, perhaps the most famous of the Greek rulers of Egypt, learned the Egyptian language, and temples throughout the land are dedicated to her and her Greek predecessors using inscriptions in Egyptian.

When the Romans conquered Cleopatra and Egypt in 30 BC, Greek continued to be used in most official documents. Despite numerous invasions and waves of peoples that have poured into our country, particularly since the Saitic (Twenty-sixth) Dynasty (664–525 BC), we Egyptians have kept our identity and traditions. Herodotus, an ancient eyewitness from Greece, was one of the first outsiders to take note of this fact in his written work: "The Egyptians avoid following Greek customs and, in general, they are unwilling to adopt customs of any people other than their own"; in another passage, he commented: "No Egyptian man or woman will kiss a Greek or use a Greek knife or spit or cauldron or even eat the flesh of a bull known to be clean, if it has been cut with a Greek knife" (Herodotus, 2.91; 41).

In short, foreigners whose intentions the Egyptians doubted were, together with their customs, unwelcome or at least accepted with much reserve. The Saitic pharaoh Amasis (570–526 BC), understanding his country's people well, initiated the wise policy of using the town of Naucratis to house the multitudes of Greek merchants who were arriving in Egypt and pressing heavily on Egyptian society. The Jews of the time likewise concentrated in a colony of their own in the far south of the country, at Elephantine, beside Aswan.

Thus, after the Greek and the later Roman conquest, educated Egyptians learned and wrote Greek, but they continued to be distinctively Egyptian and especially they continued to speak Egyptian, albeit infused with some Greek words. As the population converted to Christianity, a new form of the written language emerged, called Coptic, which represented the colloquial language that descended from the ancient tongue.

The Coptic alphabet is based on the Greek alphabet (which includes vowels, by the way), and for sounds not represented by Greek letters new ones derived from Demotic (and thus ultimately from hieroglyphs) were added at the end of the alphabet. These letters are: *shai, fai, khai, hori, jenja, chima, ti.*

Shai, used for the sound *sh* (as in *shin* or *shut)*, originally came from the hieroglyphic sign for a pool with lotus flowers that was then simplified in Demotic and further simplified in Coptic:

 → ϣ

Fai was the hieroglyphic alphabetic sign for the *f* sound, originally depicted as a horned viper:

 → ϥ

Khai was originally a single lotus plant, representing the two sounds *ḫꜣ* in Egyptian, the first consonant of which is the same sound in Coptic, a guttural sound similar to the *ch* in Scottish *loch*:

 → ϧ

Hori, representing a kind of 'breathy' *h* sound (*ḥ*), a little stronger than the *h* in *hope*, was originally an elephant tusk over a papyrus roll:

 → ϩ

Jenja represents a sound like the *j* in *judge*. *Jenja* was an ancient tool for starting a fire or a pestle with its mortar jar:

 → ϫ

Chima probably had a sound like the *cu* in *cute* or *cue:*

 → ϭ

Finally, *ti*, although it seems to be just an altered Greek *tau* (τ) actually derived from a Demotic sign that combined two commonly used hieroglyphic signs, an arm holding what is thought to be a small loaf and another sign depicting bread:

 → ϯ

It seems to have been just a shorthand for ⲧ and ⲓ, sounding together like the word *tea.*

Coptic, the last phase of the Egyptian language, survived as a living language until the seventeenth century of our present era in some villages in Upper Egypt. The Coptic Church still celebrates parts of its mass in Coptic. The Egyptians, whether Orthodox Copts or other Christians or Muslims, despite their deep-rooted religious zeal, inherited strong traditions that led them to continue to unconsciously adopt old personal names, unaware that these names were pagan and imply high esteem of ancient gods and idols.

For example, even today parents will name their sons *Banūb* بانوب, 'he who belongs to the god Anubis' (ⲠⲀⲚⲞⲨⲠ,  *pꜣ inpw*), or *Bahūr*

باهور, 'he who belongs to Horus' (ⲠⲀϨⲞⲢ,  *p3 n ḥr*).

In this brief survey of our present Egyptian linguistic inheritance, let's begin with the most popular of current ancient words in our modern life— آه *āh* (or أيوه, *aywa*), meaning 'yes.' For philologists of ancient Egyptian, "it appears to have a vague exclamatory or interjectional force . . . it seems to have some such meaning as 'indeed'" (Gardiner, § 245, p. 184), which fits perfectly with its usage today.

Many words may actually go back to the most ancient tongue, but not every word ever spoken by the Egyptian people—or even the pharaoh himself—was recorded. So sometimes we find only the traces of these ancient words in the Coptic descendant words.

With the advent of the Arabs and the expansion of Islam, the Egyptians, then known as Copts, started speaking Arabic together with their native language Coptic. The mixture of the two languages has given birth in the long run to the sweetest Arabic dialect in the Arab world today. It has also given birth to a number of expressions and idioms taken directly and translated word for word from ancient Egyptian, thus underlining the tight links with the past that remained constant over thousands of years.

Because the ancient Egyptian and Arabic languages belong to the same Hamito-Semitic family, it is sometimes difficult to discern pure Egyptian words from pure Arabic words. And some words of our modern spoken language are composed half and half of Coptic and Arabic syllables. *Ṣughannan*, for instance, meaning ‘little,’ has a first half from Arabic *ṣaghīr*, and a second half from Coptic *nun* (from ⲚⲞⲨⲚⲈ(ⲞⲨ) *nnỉ*, meaning ‘child’). This phenomenon is common in many place names and towns, particularly those beginning with *mīt* ميت Coptic ⲘⲞⲈⲒⲦ, ‘way,’ such as *Mīt Ghamr* and *Mīt Abu al-Kōm*. Coptic ϮⲘⲈ *timê* meaning ‘town’ is also frequently used either alone or in some combination, for example, *Ṭima* طما, *Ṭamāy* طماي, and Timayy تميّ. Some place names, of course, are entirely from ancient Egyptian, such as *Aswān* اسوان, a large city in Upper Egypt, from the Egyptian word for ‘trade,’ *sewen,* because the city was a center of trade: ⲤⲞⲨⲀⲚ *swnt*.

Other idioms and grammatical expressions are still distinctive: our negative *mish* مش, meaning ‘not,’ can be traced back to an ancient root: ⲘⲈϢⲈ *bw rḫ*. The same is true of our word *tannuh* تنّه, which now means ‘cause to go’ or ‘start,’ from ⲦⲚⲚⲞⲞⲨ *dỉt ỉn.w*, meaning ‘cause that they bring.’

The *ma* prefixed to the modern Egyptian verb to form the imperative is probably a Coptic inheritance: *ma-tishtaghal!* ماتشتغل ‘get to work!’ from ⲘⲀⲢⲈ ‘let (us go).’

The particle *ʿād* عاد at the end of a modern Upper Egyptian negated sentence no doubt goes back to Coptic ⲁⲛ and Egyptian  *ʿn*, for example in *mish ʿawiz ḥāja ʿād* مش عاوز حاجه عاد 'I don't want anything at all.' In this example we see evidence of a phonetic transformation that took place over time. Here the *n* of Egyptian and Coptic became pronounced as *d* in Arabic; several such transformations took place.

Finally, it is worth mentioning that the Arabic word *dahabiya* ذهبية is the name given to a kind of floating house still seen along the banks of the Nile. The word probably came from the ancient Egyptian word for ship,  *dpt,* though it was influenced by a superficial resemblance with the Arabic word for 'gold,' *dahab* ذهب. There may also be the underlying tradition of Kamose, who said he attacked the Hyksos in "his ship of gold," glossed by Professor John Wilson as a royal *dahabiya* (ANET, p. 573, n. 7).

The Ancient Egyptian Alphabet

Ancient Egyptian hieroglyphs incorporated several types of signs to represent the sounds of the ancient Egyptian language. Some signs represented what they depicted, so for example the picture of the sun 𓇳, called *rʿ* in Egyptian, was one way of writing the word *rʿ* meaning sun (such signs are often called *ideograms*, from the Greek *ideo-* 'form, shape, idea,' and *gram*, a 'writing'). The same sign could be used at the end of other words to indicate the general 'category' that the word fell into. For example, to write 'day,' *hrw* in ancient Egyptian, a concept that involves the passing of the sun through the sky, ordinary alphabetic signs for *hrw* were followed by the same sun sign at the end; this *determinative* clarified for the reader that the *hrw* the writer was talking about was the one having to do with the sun, 'day.' Sometimes signs could be used to represent the sound of the name of the objects they depicted without any associated idea. An example of such a *phonogram* is 𓇔, *wbn*, meaning 'sunrise'; it is used in the word 𓇔𓏌𓏲𓐎 *wbnw*, which includes the same sounds as the word for sunrise, but means 'wound,' an idea that has nothing to do with the sun and its rising. There are too many ideograms, determinatives, and phonograms to list them all here, but the final class of signs are *alphabetic*—used much like our Arabic and English alphabetic symbols—and a list of them follows.

Sign	**Transliteration**	**Pronunciation**
𓄿	*ꜣ*	a glottal stop; similar to Arabic *alif*
𓇋	*ỉ*	usually consonantal *y*
𓇌 or 𓏭	*y*	*y*
𓂝	*ʿ*	a guttural sound not found in English; like Arabic *ʿayn*
𓅱	*w*	*w*
𓃀	*b*	*b*
𓊪	*p*	*p*
𓆑	*f*	*f*
𓅓	*m*	*m*
𓈖	*n*	*n*
𓂋	*r*	*r*
𓉔	*h*	*h* as in English *house*
𓎛	*ḥ*	emphatic *h*; Arabic *ḥa* ح
𓐍	*ḫ*	like *ch* in Scottish *loch*; Arabic *kha* خ
𓄡	*ẖ*	a sound between *ḫ* and French or German *r*

𓊃 or 𓋴	*s*	*s* or *z*
𓈙	*š*	*sh* as in shall
𓈎	*ḳ*	like Arabic *qāf* ق
𓎡	*k*	*k*
𓎼	*g*	hard *g* as in *go*
𓏏	*t*	*t*
𓍿	*ṯ*	originally *tsh*, later like *t*
𓂧	*d*	*d*
𓆓	*ḏ*	originally *dj* or a dull emphatic *s*, later like *d*

The Coptic Alphabet

The Coptic alphabet is adapted from the Greek alphabet; several letters of the Greek alphabet represent sounds that were rare in Coptic, and as a result these letters tend to occur primarily in words of Greek origin. In the case of other letters, scholars may use a conventional pronunciation that differs from what they now believe was the actual, historical pronunciation.

Letter	**Pronunciation**
ⲁ	like *a* in *father*
ⲃ	originally *b* but nowadays pronounced *v*
ⲅ	hard *g* as in go
ⲇ	*d*
ⲉ	short *e*, as in *let*
ⲍ	*z*
ⲏ	probably like *a* in *hate*
ⲑ	*th* as in *thin*
ⲓ	like *i* in *machine*
ⲕ	*k*
ⲗ	*l*

ⲙ	*m*
ⲛ	*n*
ⲝ	a combination of *k* and *s*, rare in Coptic
ⲟ	short *o*, as in *dog*
ⲡ	*p*
ⲣ	*r*
ⲥ	*s* as in *see*
ⲧ	*t*
ⲩ	appears with other vowels in Coptic, such as ⲟⲩ, like *oo* of *food*
ⲫ	combination of *p* and *h*
ⲭ	combination of *k* and *h*
ⲯ	combination of *p* and *s*
ⲱ	long *o*, like *o* in *hope*
ϣ	*sh* as in *shall*
ϥ	*f*
ϧ	like *ch* in Scottish *loch*; Arabic *kha* خ
ϩ	emphatic *h*; Arabic *ḥa* ح

ϫ	*j* as in *judge*
ϭ	*ch* as in *church*
ϯ	the normal way to write the sounds *t* and *i* together

Another orthographic device commonly used in modern Coptic texts (not used in this book) is the period (.) to separate the definite article, ⲡ. (or ⲡⲉ.) for the masculine and ⲧ. (or ⲧⲉ.) for the feminine, from the noun root, for example, ⲡ.ⲓϧ, literally, 'the demon,' or 'the spirit,' pronounced *pikh*.

The Arabic Alphabet

The letters of the Arabic alphabet, unlike those of the Roman alphabet, which is used for representing English sounds, appear in several different forms depending on their position in the word. That is, a letter usually has different forms for when it is at the beginning of a word, when it is in the middle, and when it is at the end. Below are the forms of the letters when they are unattached.

The Arabic language also has two usual means of expression: the formal 'Classical' form that is used throughout the entire Arabic-speaking world, and informal, colloquial dialects of each Arab nation. The transliterations used in this book reflect the Egyptian spoken dialect. Certain regional variations are noted—the *j* sound of standard Arabic and of Upper Egypt is pronounced with a hard *g* sound in Cairo and other northern areas of the country. Likewise, the *q* sound of Classical Arabic is often pronounced as a glottal stop in the north and as a hard *g* in Upper Egypt.

Letter	Transliteration	Pronunciation
أ	'	*a*, *i*, or *u* depending on following vowel
ب	*b*	as in English
ت	*t*	like ordinary English *t*, as in *top*

ث	*th*	*th* as in *think*; in Egypt, often pronounced *t* or *s*
ج	*j*	*j* in the south, hard *g* in parts of the north
ح	*ḥ*	an emphatic *h*, somewhat stronger and more guttural than the *h* in *hope*
خ	*kh*	like *ch* in Scottish *loch*
د	*d*	as in *dog*
ذ	*dh*	*th* as in *though*, often pronounced *d* or *z*
ر	*r*	as in *rain*
ز	*z*	as in *zebra*
س	*s*	as in *see*
ش	*sh*	as in *shall*
ص	*ṣ*	an emphatic *s*, somewhat like *s* in *soften*
ض	*ḍ*	an emphatic *d*, somewhat like *d* in *dawdle*
ط	*ṭ*	an emphatic *t*, somewhat like *t* in *torn*

ظ	*ẓ*	an emphatic *z*, somewhat like *z* in *zoo*
ع	ʿ	*ʿayn,* a guttural sound unknown to English
غ	*gh*	the voiced equivalent of *kh*
ف	*f*	as in English
ق	*q*	an emphatic *k* sound, somewhat like *c* in *caw*
ك	*k*	as in *kin*
ل	*l*	as in English
م	*m*	as in English
ن	*n*	as in English
ه	*h*	similar to English *h*, as in *have*
و	*w*	like *w* in wave or like *oo* in *moon*
ي	*y*	like *y* in *year*; *ee* in *see*; or *a* in *malign*

2

Bayūmi

Every year, for thousands of years, the flood season, **dimīra**, initiated a happy cycle. The flood would bring about the resumption of agriculture, and it stimulated a new burst of economic and social activities in Egypt. Even now, after the building of the Aswan High Dam has reduced the impact of the annual flood, the patterns of agricultural life remain the same. Early at dawn, when the dry thirsty land, **sharāqi**, has received enough irrigated water, the peasant—we'll call him **Bayūmi**—goes out to his field, his hoe, **ṭūrya**, on his shoulder, a whip, **amsha**, in hand, driving his oxen loaded with a big sack, **shikāra**, full of seeds, probably for beans, **fūl**. Following a few steps behind Bayūmi is his donkey and her young one, a **jaḥsh**. She is loaded on each side with a basket, **shinf**, of clover, **barsīm**. On his way, Bayūmi passes a gang of laborers digging a new canal; they are encouraging each other in the work by singing **hōb, hōb, ya shughl al-nōb**. ('Work, work! Work is gold!'). Nearby are some villagers molding

dimīra	دميرة from ⲦⲈⲘⲈⲢⲈ *t3 mrỉ,* 'land of reeds'
sharāqi	شراقي from ϢⲀⲢⲔⲈ from *šrr*, 'to be little,' and *k3*, 'nourishment'
Bayūmi	بيومي from ⲠⲒⲞⲘ *p3 (n) ym,* 'he of the river or sea'
ṭūrya	طورية from ⲦⲰⲢⲈ *tr*
amsha	أمشة from ⲀⲘϢⲈ *mḫ3*
shikāra	شكارة from ϢⲔⲒⲖ *škr*
fūl	فول from ⲪⲈⲖ *pr*
jaḥsh	جحش from ϬϨⲞⲤ *gḥs*
shinf	شنف from ϪⲚⲞϤ *ḫnft*
barsīm	برسيم from ⲂⲒⲢⲤⲒⲘ *brsm*

hōb, hōb, ya shughl al-nōb هوب هوب ياشغل النوب

a combination of Arabic and Egyptian: ϨⲰⲂ ϨⲰⲂ ... ⲚⲞⲨⲂ from *h3b* ... *nb*, 'work! ... gold' and *shughl* شغل , 'work' (there is another old Egyptian word, ϨⲞⲠ from *ḥb*, meaning 'feast,' that makes one wonder about the real etymology of the *hōb* of the song) crude mud bricks, called *ṭūb* (singular **ṭuba**), from the earth thrown aside by the canal diggers.

Once Bayūmi has reached his field, he spends the early part of the morning plowing up his plot of land; he then sets his ox free from its yoke, **nāf**. When he looks around, nearly everyone in the fields around him is carrying a small basket, called a **baqūṭi**, from which they take handfuls of seeds to spread in the newly plowed ground. The sowing season has begun.

At midday, Bayūmi usually takes a break for a light lunch. In the shade of an acacia tree, **sanṭ**, he crouches on a mat, **bursh**, to eat his simple food: bread, **battāw**, cheese, **ḥalūm**, some pieces of salt turnip, **lift**, a bundle, **shirsh**, of onions and some greens, **shakūrya**, that he has rinsed, **shaṭaf**, in water. He takes care that no fly, **ʿaff**, lands on his food. He may end his meal with a handful of dates, **binni**, that he snatches from a cluster, **subāṭa**, on a nearby palm. He must be careful in climbing this skyscraper of a tree or he will fall, **yaṭubb**, quivering and shaking, **yifarfar**, on the way down. The mixed remains of his meal, **karta**, he keeps to feed his chickens.

Toward sunset, he is no doubt exhausted and scorched, **mashbūḥ**, from the day's toil and the hot weather, **shōb**. He takes his time in returning home, first putting on his clothes, **ḥabāyiṣ**. He starts driving his oxen homeward by humming a song, **yidandin**, using the traditional introduction of almost every ṭūba طوبة from ⲧⲱⲃⲉ *dbt* (this word is still used in Spanish, *adobe*, and it has been borrowed from Spanish into English)

nāf ناف from ⲛⲁϩⲃⲉϥ *nḥb.f*

baqūṭi بقوطي from ⲡⲕⲟⲧ *pꜣ ḳd*

sanṭ سنط from ϣⲟⲛⲧⲉ *šnḏt*

bursh برش from ⲡⲱⲣϣ and *prḫ*

battāw بتّاو from ⲡⲁⲧⲁⲩ *pꜣ tw*

ḥalūm حلوم from ϩⲁⲗⲱⲙ

lift لفت from ⲗⲁⲡⲧ or ⲗⲁⲧⲡ

shirsh شرش from ϣⲣⲁϣ *ḫrs*

shakūrya شكوريا from ϣⲟⲩⲕⲣⲉ *šꜣwḳr*

shaṭaf شطف from ⲥⲱⲧϥ *stf*

ʿaff عفّ from ⲁϥ *ʿf*

binni بنّي from ⲃⲛⲛⲉ *bnri*

subāṭa سُباطة from ⲥⲡⲁϯ, meaning *lips*, from *spt*

yaṭubb يطب from ϩⲧⲟⲡ *ḥdb*

yifarfar يفرفر from ϥⲣϥⲉⲣ *brbr*

karta كرتة from ⲕⲉⲣⲏⲧ, from Demotic *ḳrṯt*, 'refuse,' 'dirt' (the word *karta* gained widespread use in Egypt during World War II, when it was applied to the refuse left behind by the British armed forces)

mashbūḥ مشبوح from ϣⲱⲃϩ *šhb*

shōb شوب from ϣⲟϩⲃ, also from *šhb*

ḥabāyiṣ حبايص from ϩⲱⲃⲥ *ḥbs*

yidandin يدندن from ϭⲛϭⲛ perhaps from *ḳnḳn*

Egyptian song, **ya lēl**. He is full of hope for a fruitful season that will fill his granary, **shōna**, with grain, **nabāri**. He has faith that no unforeseen thing will destroy, **yaʿukk**, his effort and turn it into an unfulfilled dream or desire, **bōsh**, and a failure, **fashūsh**. "Only God knows," he says, "how much my harvest will measure in **ardab** and **wēba**."

Later, during the harvest season, Bayūmi will set down his scythe, **manjal**, so he can take a handful of grain from a high heap to examine as a sample, **shishni**. "Wonderful," he says, but it depends, **al-rakk**, on the quality. But he thinks that he will earn enough money, and his mind is tickled, **yizaqzaq**, with the idea of building a new house of baked bricks, with shuttered windows, **shīsh**, that overlook the main lane, **hāra**.

He is suddenly taken away from his daydreams by the insane, stolid loafer who keeps calling to him, **y-ala!**–"hey, young boy!" He remains silent as if deaf, **aṭrash**, too frightened to utter a word before this man who is perennially senselessly drunk, *sakrān* **ṭīna**, who disgustingly spits, **yitaftif**, loudly blows his nose, **yiniff**, stammers, **yitahtih**, and even breaks wind, **yijayyaṣ**, in front of everybody.

Bayūmi goes straight home, passing by the mosque and several shops. On his way, he greets the sheikh sitting ready in his long **kakūla** overcoat on top of his ya lēl يا ليل from ⲗⲟⲩⲗⲁⲓ 'to shout (with joy)'

shōna شونة from ϣⲉⲩⲛⲉ *šnwt*

nabāri نباري from ⲛⲁⲡⲣⲉ *npry*

yaʿukk يعك from ⲁⲕⲱ *3ḳ*

bōsh بوش from ⲡⲟⲩϣϣ *wḫ3*,

fashūsh فشوش from ⲡϣϣϣ *p3 ḫ3ḫ3*

ardab اردب from ⲉⲣⲧⲟⲃ

wēba ويبة from ⲟⲓⲡⲉ *ipt*

manjal منجل from ⲙⲁⲛϭⲁⲗⲉ, from Greek μάκελλα

shishni شِشني from ϣⲁϣⲛⲓ *sḫn*, 'look for, examine'

al-rakk الرَك from ⲣⲓⲕⲉ 'inclination' *rḳʿ*

yizaqzaq يزقزق from ϫⲟⲕϫⲕ from the Demotic *ḏḳʿ*, 'to tickle or tease

shīsh شيش from ϣⲟⲩϣⲧ *sšd*

hāra حارة from ϩⲓⲣ *ḫ3rw*.

y-ala! contracted from *ya-ʿayyil* ياعيّل from ⲁⲗⲟⲩ and Demotic *ʿlw*, 'child, boy'

aṭrash أطرش from ⲧⲣⲟⲟⲩϣ, 'he who does not care', from *iwty* (negative pronoun) plus *rwš*, 'to care'

ṭīna طينة from ϯϩⲉ or ⲑⲓϧⲓ *tḫ*

yitaftif يتفتف from ⲑⲟϥⲧⲉϥ *tftf*

yiniff ينف from ⲛⲓϥⲓ *nf*

yitahtih يتهته from ⲧⲁϩⲧϩ *tḫtḫ* 'to be confused'

yijayyaṣ يجيّص from ϫⲟⲕⲥⲓ or ϭⲁⲧⲥⲉ

kakūla كاكولة from ⲕⲟⲩⲕⲗⲁ from Greek κουκούλλιον, a hood or cowl of monks jallabiya and waiting under the mosque's awning for the muezzin (the man who calls Muslims to prayer). The watchman also waits, a rod, nabbūt, and a bundle, libsha, of sugarcane in his hand. He rests on a crude brick seat known as a maṣṭaba.

He passes a metal shop, where he spots his friend Qulta, using tongs, kallāba, as he removes an iron part from a hot furnace for one of the villagers' tractors.

Qulta's son meanwhile hammers a stout iron chisel, ajana, into a side wall in the shop to make a window.

Once Bayūmi reaches home, he greets his wife—let's call her Sawsan—and she tells him about her day as they share an early evening meal.

jallabiya جلابية from ϭⲟⲗⲃⲉ *grb*

nabbūt نبوت from *nbit*

libsha لبشة from ⲗⲉⲃϣ

maṣṭaba مصطبة from *mstpt,* 'box'

Qulta قلتة from ⲕⲉⲗⲗⲟϫ, 'puppy,' ' *krt̲* or *ḳrd*

kallāba كلابة from ϭⲗⲱⲃⲓ

ajana اجنة from ⲱϫⲛ, Demotic ʿ*d̲n*, 'to destroy'

Sawsan سوسن from ϣⲱϣⲉⲛ *sšn*, 'lily' or 'lotus'

3

Sawsan

While Bayūmi labors in the field, Sawsan spends her day full of activity around the house. She prepares the daily food for the family, and she has a young infant, **nūnu**, who takes a lot of her time and attention. When a child is born to an Egyptian family, it is a cause for great joy and celebration. The new arrival is often given a name our most ancient ancestors would find familiar, such as Banūb or Bahūr, which we saw above. Other popular names that come from the ancient past include **Wīṣa**, probably from the god Bes, a divinity particularly popular in the late Greco-Roman period. **Bīsa**, on the other hand, is probably from the name of the cat goddess Bastet, whose popularity was at its peak in Roman Egypt. Then there are **Bakhūm**, **Shenūda**, **Bishāy**, **Bisāda**, **Qulta** or **Qilāda**, **Swēḥa**, and **Sharābi** or **Shirbi**.

The names that have been preserved throughout the long passage of the millennia are predominantly those of boys. Among the names mentioned so far, only nūnu نونو from ⲚⲞⲨⲚⲈ(ⲞⲨ) *nnỉ*

Wīṣa ويصا from ⲂⲈⲤ *bs*, the god Bes

Bīsa بيسا from ⲂⲒⲤⲀ *bꜣstt*

Bakhūm باخوم from ⲠⲀϦⲰⲘ *pꜣ ꜥḥm*, 'god's image'

Shenūda شنودة from ϢⲈⲚⲞⲨⲦⲈ *ꜥnḫ nṯr*, 'God lives'

Bishāy بشاي from ⲠϢⲞⲒ *pꜣ šꜣi*, 'fate, destiny'

Bisāda بساده from ⲠⲤⲀⲦⲈ *pꜣ sṯt*, 'the light'

Qulta, Qilāda قلته ، قلادة from ⲔⲈⲖⲖⲞϪ *krṯ*, 'puppy'

Swēḥa سويحة from Ⲥ̇ⲞⲞⲨϨⲈ *swḥt*, 'egg'

Sharābi, Shirbi شرابي، شربي from ϢⲞⲢⲠ, 'first,' cf. ϢⲞⲢⲠ Ⲙ̄ ⲘⲒⲤⲒ *ḫrp n msy*, 'firstborn'

Sawsan and the nickname Bīsa are given to girls, but as if to make up for the shortage in Egypt, the former name is now used all over the world in many languages, including English—Susan. It may be that girls' names are subject more to fashion trends, because today there is a resurgence of ancient Egyptian names like **Isis**, **Nufret**, **Nefertiti**, **Nefertari**, and its equivalent in Arabic **Ḥalawit-hum**.

Sawsan and Bayūmi decided to name their son after Bayūmi's father, **Jamjūm** (also pronounced *Gamgūm*), but since the boy is still a baby Sawsan sometimes calls him her **nannūs**, her 'beautiful one.'

The Egyptians of today are the only people to my knowledge who, when first talking to their infant children, unconsciously first use the language of their most ancient ancestors. Jamjūm, for example, is encouraged to take his early stumbling steps with the word **tāta**. Bayūmi and Sawsan cajole him into drinking with the word **umbū**, and into eating with the word **mam**. When Jamjūm finishes his food or has had enough, he says **baḥḥ**. Sawsan feels happy to see Jamjūm grow into a well-nourished child, fat and full-bellied. She may tenderly pull him by his hair, **shūsha**, pat his back in love, **tiṭabṭab** *'alayh*, and embrace him, **ta'abbaṭ** *'alayh*. Or she may call him from a little distance, holding her arms wide open, saying, "Walk, walk, who's coming to me?" **ḥaba, ḥaba, mīn yigīni**, and Jamjūm will come

Isis إيزيس from *ist*

Nufret نفرت from *nfrt*, 'the beautiful one'

Nefertiti نفرتيتي from *nfrt iti*, 'the beautiful one has come'

Nefertari نفرتاري from *nfrt.iry*, 'their beautiful one'

Ḥalawit-hum حلوتهم, 'their beautiful one'

Jamjūm جمجوم from ϫⲉⲙϫⲟⲙ, 'strong'

nannūs ننوس from ⲛⲁⲛⲟⲩⲥ *n3 ʿn.s*, literally 'she is beautiful'

tāta تاتا from ϯϯ. *(titi)*, 'tread, pace,' from *titi*

umbū امبو from ⲙⲡⲙⲟⲟⲩ *m p3 mw*, 'from the water'

mam مم from ⲙⲁⲟⲩⲱⲙ from *my wnm*, 'give to eat'

baḥḥ بَح from ⲡⲱϩ *pḥ*, 'to reach or come to an end'

shūsha شوشة from ϫⲓϫⲱⲓ *d̠3d̠3*, 'head'

tiṭabṭab تطبطب perhaps from *t̠bt̠bt*

taʿabbaṭ تعبّط from ϩⲟⲡⲧ· *ḥpt*

ḥaba, ḥaba, mīn yigīni حبا حبا مين يجيني from ϩⲟⲡϩⲉⲡ *hbhb*, 'tread, trample' running toward her, throwing himself at her breast shouting "Boo!" **bikh!**, and she answers with an expression of fright, **ya bāy!** Then she starts lulling him, **tihannin**, in her arms. If he should fall and suffer a light wound, particularly one that swells or bubbles up, **yiba'ba'**, she turns all her attention to soothing him. She may entertain him or calm him to sleep by shaking a small rattle or bell, **jiljil**. This *jiljil* is also used in our expression 'a scandal spread with bell-ringing' *bi-jalājil*, as is practiced in popular markets, meaning that it spreads high and loud.

A few years later, Jamjūm may be punished for some mistake or disobedience. Sawsan then inflicts a light beating on him, a **sakhkha**. Later, to make up for it, she may offer him something to play with, for example, a ball. The Coptic word for ball is still used in our Egyptian dialect of Arabic, but it is applied now only to the specific ball used in shot-put, called the **julla**.

If the day is especially hot, Sawsan might give Jamjūm a bath. She dries him off with a towel, **fūṭa**, and dresses him in a clean shirt, **shāya**.

While Jamjūm is napping, Sawsan begins to make the evening's meal. Normally she cooks the food in a metal pot shaped a little like a wok, called a **ḥalla**, and she kneads the bread dough in a type of mortar called a **majūr**. She has to pay great attention while kneading that she does not leave any lump, **kalkū'a**, in the dough bikh — بخ from ⲡⲓϧ, 'the demon,' from *p3 3ẖ*, 'the spirit'

ya bāy — ياباي from ⲃⲁⲓ *b3*, 'night raven,' 'screech owl'

tihannin — تهنن from ϩⲗⲟⲟⲗⲉ *hnhn*,

yiba'ba' — يبأبأ from ⲃⲉⲉⲃⲉ *b3b3i*

jiljil — جلجل from ϭⲏⲗ

sakhkha — سخّة from ⲥⲱϣ *sẖ*

julla — جلة from ϭⲁⲟⲓ ϭⲱⲁ

fūṭa — فوطة from ϥⲱⲧⲉ *fṯy*

shāya — شاية perhaps from *ḏ3yt*

ḥalla — حله from ϩⲛⲁⲩ *ḥnw*

majūr — مجور from ⲙⲁⲕⲣⲟ cf. *mḳr*, 'vessel'

kalkū'a — كلكوعة from ⲕⲉⲗⲕⲟⲩⲗⲉ or ⲕⲗⲕⲁ cf. *k3k3wt*

that would stiffen the bread and make it inedible. *Kalkūʿa* is also applied metaphorically to little problems or any slight uneasiness.

Sawsan has two older sisters—whom we'll call **Sūna** and **Dōsa**—and they often come to visit her as she is preparing bread and cleaning vegetables. Sūna is now a widow with three children, and she often complains to Sawsan of being too overburdened to carry, **titill**, her accumulating, **titkabbib**, responsibilities toward her children.

Dōsa is divorced from a man whom we'll call Sharābi. She discovered—too late—that she had fallen into the hands of a rapacious imposter, **nūri**, who took advantage of her ignorance. "This is why, **atāri**," says Sawsan to Dōsa, "he kept going around, **yiḥamḥam**, so long deceiving you." Dōsa uses a pin, **dabbūs**, to jab into a paper doll that represents Sharābi and she recites certain spells she's learned that are believed to be effective in confusing, **titwil**, the man she detests.

Dōsa regularly reports to Sawsan on her efforts against Sharābi. Whenever she sees him, Dōsa attacks, **tilkush**, Sharābi with a stream of harsh insults, **sharshaḥa**, and recently she has even resorted to sorcery. Unfortunately, poor Dōsa has fallen into the hands of a woman who has convinced her through deceit or a lie, **fahlawa**, that she is able to cast a spell, **shabshaba**, against her enemy.

Sūna سونة, a woman's nickname, from ⲥⲱⲛⲉ *snt*, 'sister'

Dōsa دوسة, a woman's nickname, from *tꜣ ist*, the goddess Isis

titill تتلّ from ⲧⲁⲗⲟ, from *rdit ꜥr*, 'to cause to ascend'

titkabbib تتكبب from ⲕⲱⲃ *ḳꜣb*, literally 'doubling'

nūri نوري from ⲛⲟⲩⲣⲉ *nrt*, literally 'vulture'

atāri أتاري from ⲉⲑⲣⲉ, *rdy.t iry*, 'cause to do (something)'

yiḥamḥam يحمحم from ϩⲟⲙϩⲉⲙ *hmhm*

dabbūs دبّوس from ⲧⲱⲃⲥ *tbs*, 'to prick'

titwil تتول from ⲑⲟⲩⲉⲗⲟ (or ⲧⲟⲩⲗⲟ) from Demotic *dy.t.ulꜥ*

tilkush تلكش from ⲗⲱⲕⲥ *nsḳ*

sharshaḥa شرشحة perhaps from ϣⲁϩϣⲉϩ, 'to be harsh, rough, hardy'

fahlawa فهلوه from ⲫⲗⲏⲟⲩ or ⲉⲡⲣⲁ, perhaps from *prt*, 'vanities'

shabshaba شبشبة from ϣⲟⲃϣⲉⲃ *ḫbḫb*

milabbish ملبّش from ⲗⲱⲃϣ

She promises to turn her luckless ex-husband into one paralyzed or fettered, **milabbish**, confused of mind, **mishawwish**, and in tatters, **mihalhil**. In short, her magic will defile, **yisakhkham**, Sharābi 's life.

mishawwish مشوّش from ϣⲱϣ,  *š3š3*, 'twisted'

mihalhil مهلهل from ϩⲟⲗϩⲗ perhaps from  *h̲nh̲n*, 'to scatter'

yisakhkham يسخّم from ϭⲱϧⲙ (or ϫⲱϩⲙ), Demotic *d̲ḫm*, 'sooty'

4

What's for Dinner?

When Sawsan offers her family various dinner dishes, she uses the same names for many foods that were used in the time of Ramesses II or Khufu, builder of the Great Pyramid. Most meals begin with bread being passed around. The modern Egyptians are perhaps the only people in the Arab world to use the word *ʿaysh* عيش , literally 'life,' for bread, as did their ancient ancestors, who used  *ʿnḫ* as a common word for bread, with the root *ʿnḫ* referring both to life and what keeps it going. We still use the metaphorical expression **akl al-ʿaysh**, literally 'eating bread,' to mean to earn one's living, just as Ptahhotep did in his maxims twenty-five centuries ago. Similarly, **al-ʿaysh inqataʿ**, 'the bread was cut off,' means that a job is lost or a relationship is broken.

The brown bread known as **sinn** was given as an offering to the gods in ancient times from at least the Middle Kingdom, and it is now appreciated by many mortals, especially those who suffer from diabetes. And

akl al-ʿaysh أكل العيش cf. ancient Egyptian 
wnm t

al-ʿaysh inqataʿ العيش انقطع

sinn سنّ from  *snw* we've already seen that Bayūmi ate a little **battāw** with cheese for lunch; *battāw* is the standard bread in the Upper Egyptian countryside.

Surveying the modern Egyptian food that Bayūmi and his family eat for ancient parallels, one finds a comparatively long list, but the beans known as **fūl** are at the top of the list, and the name is virtually unchanged. *Fūl* has been and still is the most popular commodity, prepared in various ways, particularly **midammis**, covered with water in a pot and left to slow cook, sometimes buried in hot sand. Other bean dishes are also known, for example, **biṣāra**, in addition to plain germinated boiled beans, preferred for the sick. **Gullāsh**, a thin bread in sheets, was singled out by Herodotus (2.77; called κυλλᾶστις) and is attested since the time of Seti II. It was described by the ancient Egyptians themselves as very tasty and it is still a favorite here, although it is now stuffed with meat or cheese. Types of bread usually made of fine white flour are known in Arabic as well as Coptic as **samīṭ**, from which is also made the round baked or fried cake called **qurṣ**, often having some sesame, **simsim**, scattered on the surface. From the Old Kingdom is attested a kind of pastry or cake that may be our famous **kunāfa**.

Sawsan flavors her food with butter and honey, **samn wa-ʿasal**, used together proverbially nowadays to

battāw بتّاو from ⲠⲀⲦⲀⲨ *pꜣ tw*

fūl فول from ⲫⲈⲖ *pr*

midammis مدّمس from ⲦⲰⲘⲤ *tms*, 'to bury'

biṣāra بصاره from ⲠⲒⲤⲈ ⲞⲨⲎⲢ perhaps from *ps-wr,* 'very cooked,' or from *ps*, 'cooking,' and *iwryt*, 'beans'

gullāsh جُلاّش from ⲔⲨⲖⲖⲎϬⲦⲒϨ *kršt*

samīṭ سميط from ⲤⲀⲘⲒⲦ from Greek σεμίδαλις, 'flour'

qurṣ قرص from ⲔⲢⲞⲨϪ 'a disk or something round'

simsim سمسم from ⲤⲒⲘⲤⲒⲘ

kunāfa كنافة from ⲔⲈⲚⲈⲫⲒⲦⲈⲚ *ḫnfw*

samn wa-ʿasal سمن وعسل

express harmony and intimacy. That proverb is translated from the Coptic, but the Coptic words themselves, **kāni wa-māni**, are also still used to express the same sentiments. The ancient word for 'honeycomb' survives in **nāni**, as a nickname for children. And the opposite taste—acid—survives as well, **ḥāmīḍ**.

Sawsan might prepare chicken or red meat, but both she and her husband love fish best of all. Various kinds of fish are known in modern Egyptian Arabic under the same Coptic names, which presumably go back to ancient Egyptian words: **būri** (mullet), **rāy**, **labīs**, **shilba**, **ramrūm** (tilapia), and **ṣīr**, a small fish eaten with salt and taken as a metaphor for extremely salty food. Sawsan and Bayūmi happen to live in Upper Egypt, near to a family of Nubians, who traditionally do not eat catfish (Egyptian  *nʿr*), saying that it had eaten their great-grandfather, and the Egyptians of today use its Arabic name **qarmūṭ** as a euphemism for 'phallus,' a fact that immediately calls to mind the myth of Osiris, whose phallus was devoured by a catfish.

After the main course, Bayūmi and his family like to eat a little fruit or maybe a cookie. Among their favorite fruits are watermelon, **baṭṭīkh**, and apples, **tuffāḥ**. A favorite Egyptian cookie, popular especially during feasts, is the **kaʿk**.

After dinner, Sawsan and Bayūmi often relax with a

kāni wa-māni كاني وماني from ⲔⲎⲚⲈ and ⲚⲎⲚⲒ *ḳny*, 'fat,' and *nnyw*, 'honey'

nāni ناني from ⲚⲎⲚⲒ *mni*

ḥāmiḍ حامض from ϨⲘϪ *ḥmḏ*, 'vinegar'

būri بوري from ⲂⲰⲢⲈ *br*

rāy راي from ⲢⲎⲒ

labīs لبيس from ⲖⲞⲂⲤ from Demotic *lbs*

shilba شلبة from ϬⲖⲂⲞⲞⲨ

ramrūm رمروم from ⲢⲀⲘⲒ *rmw*, 'fish'

ṣīr صير from ϪⲒⲢ

qarmūṭ قرموط

baṭṭīkh بطيخ from *bddkꜣ*

tuffāḥ تفاح from ϪⲘⲠⲈϨ, var. ϪⲠⲞϨ, *ḏpḥ*

kaʿk كعك from ⲔⲀⲀⲔⲈ *kʿk*

calming cup of tea with mint or just a cup of anise, **aysūn**. Among Egyptians, particularly of Aswan, the new beer called **marīsa** is also popular, drunk usually from a big cup called a **shubb**.

aysūn ايسون perhaps from ⲁⲃⲥⲱⲛ  *ỉbsꜣ*, 'mint' (today this word has come to designate anise rather than mint)

marīsa مريسة from ⲙⲣⲓⲥ  *mrsw*

shubb شُبّ from ϫⲟⲡ  *ṯꜣb*

5

Neighborhood Characters

After dinner, Bayūmi decides to visit his uncle Banūb, who lives nearby. When he arrives he discovers several of his uncle's friends already gathered there talking about some of the neighborhood lowlife. Each one is telling about the worst behavior they've ever experienced. They all agree they'd like to simply sweep away in a plague, **shōṭa**, all the hated people or the unruly mob, **ḥawash**.

Banūb, however, has a story to tell about mean behavior that tops all the other accounts. That very day, in horror and disgust, he witnessed a neighborhood bully inflicting harsh, heavy-handed blows, **īd ṭursha**, on his weak and lean apprentice, **mashmūm**, who was jumping, **yufuṭṭ**, from the pain and crying aloud for rescue, **jāy!**

On seeing the cruelty, Banūb ran to the shop of the torturer and denounced him as a dirty, abominable creature of base or notorious character, an **ʿifish**. While Banūb was still criticizing the man, the poor lad, quite shōṭa شوطة from ϣⲱⲱⲧ  *šʿd*, ‘massacre, catastrophe, epidemic’

ḥawash حَوش from ϩⲟⲟⲩϣ from Demotic *ḥwš*, which meant literally ‘cursed’

īd ṭursha ايد طرشة from Arabic *īd*, ‘hand,’ and ⲧⲱⲣϣ, perhaps from  *dšr*, ‘to be red (with anger?)’

mashmūm مشموم from ϣⲏⲙ  *ḫmꜣꜣ*, ‘small person, thing, or quantity’

yufuṭṭ يفّط from ⲡⲱⲧ from  *pd* or  *ftft*, ‘to run, or run away’

jāy جاي from ⲟⲩϫⲁⲓ  *wḏꜣ*

ʿifish عفش from ⲉⲡϣⲉ  *ʿpšꜣyy*, ‘cockroach, or other unpleasant insect’ breathless, **makrūsh al-nafas**, took refuge in a corner and sat neglected, **mitlaqqaḥ**, groaning, **yiwaḥwaḥ**. Banūb and the man continued to discuss the proper treatment of hired workers for some time, while the boy crept away. To the overheated, **mizafzif**, bully, Banūb at last gave the following advice: "Be careful! Anyone treated too severely may rebel, **yibawwij**, and boil and bubble, **yibaʿbaʿ**, with fury and disturbance, **habhaba**. A better approach would be to study his temperament, **yishūf khīmuh**, an expression perhaps influenced by the routine measurements made of the level of the Nile, especially during the flood season, to study its progress. The same concept of checking someone's temperament or mood by comparing the mood to water is found in a variety of other expressions, including Sinuhe's words:

ỉr bw nfr n ḫꜣst wnnty.sy ḥr mw.f

"(he will not fail to) do good to a country that will be on his water," that is, loyal to him, according to his mood. The same meaning is found in the Egyptian Arabic expression, 'to be on someone's water,' **yikūn ʿala mayyit fulān**.

Banūb and his assembled friends agree that the bully is plainly unwise in his treatment of his apprentice.

makrūsh al-nafas مكروش النفس from ⲕⲱⲣϫ, 'in a broken state,' and Arabic *nafas*, 'breath'

mitlaqqaḥ متلقح from ⲗⲁⲕϩ  *rkꜥ*, 'corner'

yiwaḥwaḥ يوحوح from ⲟⲩⲁϩⲃⲉϥ  *wḥwḥ*

mizafzif مزفزف from ϫⲟϥϫϥ  *d̠fd̠f*

yibawwij يبوّج from ⲃⲟϭⲥ  *bgs*

yibaʿbaʿ يبعبع from ⲃⲉⲉⲃⲉ  *bꜣbꜣy*

habhaba هبهبه from ϩⲟⲡϩⲡ  *hbhb*

yishūf khīmuh يشوف خيمه from Arabic *yishūf*, 'to see,' and ϩⲁⲙⲉ

yikūn ʿala mayyit fulān يكون على ميّة فلان

They describe him as **ṭurubsh**, a stupid or dull person, since he didn't listen to Banūb's sound advice. The same root also provides us with **tirbās**, a person of dubious character or a conspirator.

ṭurubsh طربش from ⲦⲈⲢⲠⲞⲤⲈ, a Demotic, *tbipsi*, literally 'baked brick'

tirbās ترباس

6

Celebration!

Bayūmi, Sawsan, and Jamjūm often attend the weekly village market day, where they might find players, dancers, snake charmers, and conjurers. These entertainers usually start their show by calling on everyone to gather around: **tūt ḥāwi**! Some of the hard-working villagers may not want the distraction immediately in their busy day, and as the crowds begin to swell in the market square, they express their displeasure at the intrusion by shouting, "Finish your work, if you want to get paid!" **shīka-bīka!**

Once a year, the Egyptian social calendar is enlivened with the celebration of *Ramaḍān*, which begins with the appearance of the crescent moon. It is really a matter of wonder that this particular new moon announcing the Islamic month of fasting was and is still celebrated in Coptic, the language used today in Egyptian Christian rituals. Children with lanterns go about the villages chanting "Welcome, welcome, o crescent," **waḥawy ya waḥawy iyūḥa**. Their

tūt ḥāwi توت حاوي from ⲦⲞⲞⲨⲦⲈ *twt,* 'to gather or collect,' and the Arabic **ḥāwi** meaning 'charmer'

shīka-bīka! شيكا بيكا from ϪⲰⲔ ϪⲒ ⲂⲈⲔⲈ from Demotic *ḏk*, 'finish,' *t3w*, 'take,' *b3k*, 'salary, work' (the whole phrase thus meant literally, "Finish (your work)! Take your salary!")

waḥawy ya waḥawy iyūḥa وحوي ياوحوي ايوحة from ⲞⲨⲰϨ ⲞⲨⲰϨ ⲒⲞϨ from *w3ḥ,* 'to stay, put,' and *iꜥḥ,* 'moon' song continues with "How sweet, how sweet," **yaḥlēla, yaḥlēla**. The celebrations are called **hawsa** and **rawsha**, but trouble, **hēṣa**, can also result.

During celebratory gatherings, a woman like Sawsan might stand up and address her friends and neighbors by shouting "Distinguished dear ladies," **shōbash ya-ḥabāyib**. To express wonder and amazement she may say "What's happening to you!" **ishbār ʿalayk!** If she is feeling overwhelmed and distressed, she may exclaim "Oh my trouble!" **ya ḥōmti!** or even "Oh my burial!" **ya kāsi!** A controversial subject is described as causing 'an inquiry and a ringing,' **shanna wa-ranna**.

Bayūmi and Sawsan organize their daily life and agricultural activities around a special calendar that has been inherited from their most ancient ancestors. Names of the months of the Coptic calendar, which came to be used alongside the Gregorian and Hegira calendars, reflect an even more ancient origin, and these names are still used, especially in the countryside. The ordinary *fellaḥīn*, or farmers, retain this calendar, unaware that the names honor gods like Thoth, Hathor, and Khonsu, nor do they allow their Christian or Muslim faith to be disturbed by such pagan names. Throughout the centuries, they have found in our ancestors' calendar an excellent chronometer that was an accurate guide for life. The names of the months in Arabic, Coptic, and Egyptian can be found over the page.

yaḫlēla, yaḫlēla يا حليلة يا حليلة from ⲉⲓⲉϩⲉⲗⲟⲟⲗ, from *ꜣḥt iꜣrr.t,* 'vineyard,' literally 'field of grapes'

hawsa هوسة from ϩⲱⲥ *ḥsy,* 'to sing'

rawsha روشة from ⲣⲁϣⲉ *ršw*, 'joy, gladness'

hēṣa هيصة from ϩⲓⲥⲉ *ẖsy*

shōbash ya-ḥabāyib شوبش يا حبايب from ϣⲁⲡϣⲓ (later written as) *špst*, 'distinguished, noble women'; *ḥabāyib* is Arabic for 'dear ones'

ishbār ʿalayk اشبار عليك from ϣⲡⲏⲣⲉ *ẖprt*, which originally meant 'event' but already in the pharaonic period came to mean 'miracle, amazing thing'

ya ḥōmti يا حومتي from ϩⲟⲉⲓⲙ *hꜣnw,* 'a wave'

ya kāsi يا كاسي from ⲕⲁⲓⲥⲉ *ḳrst*

shanna wa-ranna شنّه ورنه from ϣⲓⲛⲉ *šny*, 'inquiry,' and Arabic *ranna*

The Months of the Ancient Calendar

Date	Arabic	
Sept/Oct	توت	*Tūt*
Oct/Nov	بابه	*Bāba*
Nov/Dec	هاتور	*Hatūr*
Dec/Jan	كيهك	*Kiyahk*
Jan/Feb	طوبة	*Ṭūba*
Feb/Mar	امشير	*Amshīr*
Mar/Apr	برمهات	*Baramhāt*
Apr/May	برمودة	*Barmūda*
May/June	بشنس	*Bashans*
Jun/July	بؤونة	*Ba'ūna*
July/Aug	أبيب	*Abīb*
Aug/Sept	مسرى	*Misra*

Coptic	**Egyptian**	
ⲐⲞⲞⲨⲦ		*ḏḥwt*
ⲠⲀⲞⲠⲈ		*pꜣ n i͗pt*
ϨⲀⲦⲰⲢ		*ḥt ḥr*
ⲔⲞⲒⲀϨⲔ		*kꜣ ḥr kꜣ*
ⲦⲰⲂⲈ		*tꜣ ꜥb*
ⲘϢⲒⲢ		*mḫyr*
ⲠⲀⲢⲘϨⲞⲦⲠ		*pꜣ n i͗mn-ḥtpw*
ⲠⲀⲢⲘⲞⲨⲦϨ		*pꜣ n rnnt*
ⲠⲀϢⲞⲚⲤ		*pꜣ n ḫnsw*
ⲠⲀⲰⲚⲈ		*pꜣ n i͗nt*
ⲈⲠⲎⲠ		*i͗pi͗p*
ⲘⲈⲤⲰⲢⲎ		*msw rꜥ*

Instructive mottos and phrases that highlighted the quality of each month or what should be done during that time were passed down from generation to generation.

Associated sayings reveal the character of the month, similar in a way to the English proverb, "March winds and April showers bring forth May flowers." And like this English counterpart, what makes these month mottos in Arabic so memorable is that they normally have an element of rhyme. Regarding the second month, for example, it is said: "**Bāba**: come in and close the door." The month of Bāba is the beginning of the cold season, hence the motto's urging to get inside and keep out the cold.

The month of Hatūr is the time when sowing begins again; before the building of the Aswan High Dam, when the floodwaters began retreating, it was time to plant, hence the saying, "**Hatūr**: of sown gold." The sown 'gold' of the expression is wheat.

The next month, Kiyahk, which corresponds to December and January, is the time when the days are shortest, so we Egyptians say "**Kiyahk**: your morning is your evening; you take your hand off your breakfast to put it on your supper." Ṭūba follows Kiyahk, and it is known for being the coldest time of the year, so cold, in fact, that "**Ṭūba** turns the old woman stiff." Some people add the comment that it makes the young

Bāba—khushsh w-iqfil al-bawāba

بـابـه خش واقفل البوابـة

Hatūr—abu al-dahab al-mantūr

هـاتور أبو الذهب المنتور

Kiyahk—ṣabāḥak masāk tishīl īdak min fuṭūrak tiḥuṭṭaha fi ʿashāk

كيهك صبـاحك مسـاك، تشيل ايدك من فطورك تحطهـا في عشـاك

Ṭūba—tikhalli al-ʿajūza ʿarqūba

طوبـة تخلي العجوزة عرقوبـة (كركوبـة والشـابـة قردة)

woman look like a monkey, because everyone gets so shriveled up from the chill!

In a similar vein to the English expression "March comes in like a lion and goes out like a lamb," Amshīr starts out with sandstorms that turn to summer breezes: "**Amshīr**: of numerous storms, but gives the feeling of summer."

Baramhāt in mid-April and May is the season of the harvest, so farmers now say of it, "**Baramhāt**: go to the field and fetch." The harvest continues in full swing the following month, the time for threshing, as we say, "**Barmūda**: pound with the rod." By the time of Bashans, the harvest is complete, there is nothing left in the field, and there is no cultivation: "**Bashans**: sweeps the fields entirely."

The motto for the following month is unusual in two ways. Firstly, it does not have a rhyme. Secondly, there is a most interesting case of misinterpretation of the ancient language. The modern farmer says, "**Ba'ūna** splits the stone," using the splitting of the stone as a metaphor for the hot weather and extreme desiccation that takes place in this month, so strong it could split a rock in two! Yet this metaphor, visually striking as it is, is based on the wrong translation of the ancient ⲱⲛⲉ (as coming from  *inr*, 'rock'). The word actually comes from a different root ( *int*), meaning 'valley,' in reference to the ancient

Amshīr—abu al-zaʿabīb al-kitīr, yikhabbaṭ yilabbaṭ fīh min rawāyiḥ al-ṣayf

امشير ابو الزعابيب الكثير، يخبّط يلبّط فيه من روايح الصيف

Baramhāt—rūḥ al-ghayṭ wa-hāt

برمهات روح الغيط وهات

Barmūda—duqq bi-l-ʿamūda

برمودة دق بالعمودة

Bashans—yuknus al-ghiṭān kans

بشنس يكنس الغيطان كنس

Baʾūna—tifliq al-hajar

بؤونة تفلق الحجر

Egyptian feast of the desert valley of Deir al-Baḥari that was celebrated in Thebes in this month. This misinterpretation gives a resounding echo of our deep Egyptian roots.

When the floodwaters begin to return in late August and early September, the comment is that "**Misra** loosens the tough earth." The waters soften the ground that had been hardened by the hot, dry summer.

Misra—yafukk al-arḍ al-ʿisra

مسرى يفك الأرض العسرة

7

Wisdom of Old

To this brief account may be added a number of sayings that are still current in our daily life:

shubbēk lubbēk

شبيك لبيك

"At your service, Your Excellency"

The first word of the expression, *shubbēk*, means in Egyptian 'your excellency,' from ϢⲂⲎ  *šfyt*; the second word, *lubbēk*, means 'here I am for you' in Classical Arabic.

aʿmil ḥisāb marīsi, wa in jāt tiyāb, min Allah

اعمل حساب مريسي وإن جات تياب من الله

"Plan as if expecting the south wind (unfavorable for sailing upstream), and if the (pleasant) east wind blows, it is from God"

The word for the south wind, *marīsi*, comes from ⲢⲎⲤ *rsy*, preceded by the preposition *m*, 'from.' The word for the east wind, *tiyāb*, comes from ⲦⲈⲒⲈⲂⲦ *tꜣ iꜣb.ty*, '(the) eastern.' The proverb is commonly used to advise people to save as if bad times were certain to come, but to thank God when the savings are not needed.

al-malāwiʿ yuqaʿ fi-arda' al-talalīs

الملاوع يقع في اردأ التلاليس

"A crook sinks in the worst mire"

In other words, no matter how sneaky a person is, sooner or later s/he will be trapped. The Arabic word for mire, *talalīs*, comes from Coptic ⲐⲰⲖⲤ̄, meaning 'mud' or 'muck.'

timla bi-l-hiriwwa, tiqill al-miriwwa

تملا بالهروّة تقل المروة

"Full of food, energy reduced"

The word *hiriwwa* is from ϨⲢⲈⲨⲈ *ẖrt*, 'food,' and the proverb is invoked to advise people not to eat too much, since when they do, they become sluggish.

tinʿi zayy al-durra

تنعي زي الدرّة

"Mourning and weeping like a kite"

The kite, ⲦⲢⲈ *ḏrt,* personified Isis and Nephthys lamenting their brother Osiris, and this expression is often used to describe the wailing and other sorrowful cries of lamentation that rural women use to express their grief when a close relative dies.

al-qamḥ taʾmīḥa

القمح تأميحة

"Wheat is death"

Said of one who dreams of wheat, in a pun between Arabic *qamḥ*, 'wheat,' and Egyptian *ỉmḥt*, 'necropolis.'

dahya tiwaddīh al-amendi

داهية توديه الامندي

"May a disaster send him to hell"

The word *amendi*, 'hell,' is from Coptic ⲀⲘⲚⲦⲈ and ultimately from Egyptian *ỉmntt*, a word used for the underworld.

jāk maw

جاك مَو

"May a lion come to you"

A pun on the words for 'lion' ⲘⲞⲒ  *mꜣy* and 'mother' ⲘⲀⲀⲨ  *mwt,* and used by mothers harassed by the demands of their children.

jāt al-ʿudwa titshalshil bi-tarḥitha tibki bi-ḥurqa min kutr farḥitha

جات العدوة تتشلشل بطرحتها تبكي بحرقة من كتر فرحتها

"The enemy woman came, pulling violently on the veil around her neck, weeping loudly, but out of joy"

The Arabic word for pulling violently on something, *shalshil,* comes from Coptic ϣⲟⲗϣⲗ. The expression is used when a woman comes to a funeral shrieking with grief, but inwardly rejoicing with delight.

jā yuhurr

جا يهر

"He came with diarrhea"

An expression used to describe someone incontinent

with fear when reporting to a superior. The word *yuhurr* comes from ϨΟΙΡΕ *ḥry*, literally 'dung.'

al-tirʿa nishfit wa-bānit zaqazīqha

الترعة نشفت وبانت زقازيقها

"The canal dried up and its small fish appeared"

This saying may be used to suggest that secrets have been divulged, or when someone asks a friend for money and that friend has nothing left to give—similar to the English expression, "The well has gone dry." *Zaqazīq*, 'small fish,' is from ϪΕΚϪΙΚ, which meant 'small.'

maqfūl bi-l-ḍabba wa-l-muftāḥ

مقفول بالضبة والمفتاح

"Closed with lock and key"

Said of something that is firmly and permanently locked up. *Ḍabba*, 'wooden lock,' is from Coptic ΤΕΠΩ, from Egyptian *tꜣ pꜣyt*.

yuḥuṭṭ al-ḥaba' wa-l-naba' wa-shūsht ummuh fi-l-ṭabaq

يحط الحبأ والنبأ وشوشة أُمّه في الطبق

"He should put his plow, his gold, and his mother's hair in the dish"

That is, in order to propose to a girl, a young man should prove—together with his own mother's consent—to be well-to-do, through possession of land and money symbolized respectively by the plow, *ḥaba'*, from ϩⲃⲃⲉ  *hb,* and gold, *naba'*, from ⲛⲟⲩⲃ  *nb.*

Glossaries

Compiled by Mary Knight

𓄿

𓄿 *3* آه *ah!* (or أيوه , *aiwa!*), 'yes'

3ḥt i3rr.t ⲉⲓⲉϩⲉⲗⲟⲟⲗ 'vineyard,' literally 'field of grapes'; found in expression ياحليلة ياحليلة *yaḥlēla, yaḥlēla,*'how sweet, how sweet'

3k ⲁⲕⲱ عك *'akk*, 'to destroy'

𓇋

i3b.ty used with article *t3* in ⲧⲉⲓⲉⲃⲧ, 'eastern,' تياب *tiyāb*, 'east wind'

ym ⲓⲟⲙ يم *yamm*, 'sea'

iʿḥ, 'moon,' origin of Coptic expression ⲟⲩⲱϩ ⲟⲩⲱϩ ⲓⲟϩ and equivalent Arabic expression وحوي ياوحوي ايوحة *waḥawy ya waḥawy iyūḥa*, 'welcome, welcome, o crescent'

iwty a negative pronoun, perhaps with *rwš*, 'to care,' was source of Arabic أطرش *aṭrash*, 'deaf'

ibs3 ⲁⲃⲥⲱⲛ, 'mint,' perhaps origin of ايسون *aysūn* a kind of anise drink *ipip* ⲉⲡⲏⲡ أبيب *Abīb* (month)

ipt ⲟⲓⲡⲉ ويبة *wēba*, a unit of measurement of dry weight

imntt ⲁⲙⲛⲧⲉ امندي *amendi*, ‘hell, the underworld’

imḥt, ‘necropolis’

inr ⲱⲛⲉ ‘rock’

int ⲱⲛⲉ, ‘valley’

ist إيزيس *Izīs*, ‘Isis’ (ancient goddess; revived as a woman’s name); with article *t3*, origin of woman’s nickname *Dōsa* دوسة

ʿf ⲁϥ عفّ *ʿaff*, ‘fly’

ʿnḫ ‘life; that which sustains life, bread’; cf. عيش *ʿaysh*

ʿnḫ nṯr ϣⲉⲛⲟⲩⲧⲉ شنودة *Shenūda* ‘God lives’ (man’s name)

ʿlw (Demotic) ⲁⲗⲟⲩ, ‘child, boy,’ used in the expression ياعيّل *ya ʿayyil* and its contracted form *y-ala!* ‘hey, young man!’

ʿn ⲁⲛ عاد *ʿād*, particle in a negative sentence

ʿḏn (Demotic) ⲱϫⲛ, ‘to destroy,’ origin of اجنة *ajana* ‘iron chisel’

w3ḥ, ‘to stay, put,’ origin of Coptic expression ⲟⲩⲱϩ ⲟⲩⲱϩ ⲓⲟϩ and equivalent Arabic expression

وحوي ياوحوي ايوحة *waḥawy ya waḥawy iyūḥa*, 'welcome, welcome, o crescent'

wbn, 'sunrise'

wbnw, 'wound'

wnm t 'eating bread; earning one's living'; cf. the Arabic expression أكل العيش *akl al-ʿaysh*

wḥwḥ ⲞⲨⲀϨⲂⲈϤ يوحوح *yiwaḥwaḥ* 'to groan'

wḫ3 used with article *p3* in ⲠⲞⲨⲰϢ بوش *bōsh*, 'dream or desire'

wḏ3 ⲞⲨϪⲀⲒ جاي *jāy*, 'cry out from pain for rescue'

b3 'soul, spirit,' used in Arabic expression of fright يا باي *ya bāy*,

b3b3i ⲂⲈⲈⲂⲈ بأبأ *baʾbaʾ*, 'to bubble up'; and بعبع *baʿbaʿ*, 'to boil'

b3stt ⲂⲒⲤⲀ بيسا *Bīsa*, 'the goddess Bastet' (woman's name)

b3k ⲂⲈⲔⲈ 'salary; work,' found in Arabic expression شيكا بيكا *shika-bika!* 'Finish your work if you want to get paid!'

bw rḫ ⲘⲈϢⲈ مش *mish*, 'not'

br ⲂⲰⲢⲈ بوري *būri*, 'mullet'

brbr ϤⲢϤⲈⲢ يفرفر *yifarfar*, 'to shake, shiver'

brsm ⲂⲒⲢⲤⲒⲘ برسيم *barsīm*, 'clover'

bnri ⲂⲚⲚⲈ بنّي *binni*, 'dates'
bgs ⲂⲞϬⲤ بوّج *bawwij*, 'to rebel'
bddk3 بطّيخ *baṭṭīkh*, 'watermelon'

□

p3 3ḫ ⲠⲒϦ بخ *bikh*, 'demon'
p3 inpw ⲠⲀⲚⲞⲨⲠ بانوب *Banūb*, 'he who belongs to the god Anubis' (man's name)
p3yt used with article *t3* in ⲦⲈⲠⲰ ضبّة *ḍabba*, 'part of the fastening of a door'
p3 ꜥḫm ⲠⲀϦⲰⲘ باخوم *Bakhūm*, 'god's image' (man's name)
p3 (n) ipt ⲠⲀⲞⲠⲈ بابه *Bāba* (month)
p3 n imn-ḥtpw ⲠⲀⲢⲘϨⲞⲦⲠ برمهات *Baramhāt* (month)
p3 (n) int ⲠⲀⲰⲚⲈ بؤونة *Ba'ūna* (month)
p3 (n) ym ⲠⲒⲰⲘ بيومي *Bayūmi*, 'he of the river or sea' (man's name)
p3 n rnnt ⲠⲀⲢⲘⲞⲨⲦϨ برمودة *Barmūda* (month)
p3 n ḫnsw ⲠⲀϢⲞⲚⲤ بشنس *Bashans* (month)
p3 n Ḥr ⲠⲀϨⲞⲢ باهور *Bahūr*, 'he who belongs to Horus' (man's name)
p3 ḫ3ḫ3 ⲠϢⲰϢ فشوش *fashūsh*, 'failure'
p3 sṯt ⲠⲤⲀⲦⲈ بساده *Bisāda*, 'the light' (man's name)

p3 š3i ⲡϣⲟⲓ بشاي *Bishāy*, 'fate or destiny' (man's name)

p3 ḳd ⲡⲕⲟⲧ بقوطي *baqūṭi*, 'small basket'

p3tw ⲡⲁⲧⲁⲩ بَتَّاو *battāw*, a kind of bread

pr ⲫⲉⲗ فول *fūl*, 'fava beans'

pr ʿ3 فرعون *firʿūn*, 'pharaoh'

and *prḫ* ⲡⲱⲣϣ برش *bursh*, 'mat'

prt 'vanities,' perhaps origin of ⲫⲗⲏⲟⲩ or ⲉⲡⲣⲁ فهلوه *fahlawa*, 'deceit'

pḥ ⲡⲱϩ بَح *baḥḥ*, 'to come to an end'

ps-wr 'very cooked'; this word or perhaps , 'cooking,' and , *iwryt*, 'beans,' is the origin of بصاره *biṣāra*, a bean dish

pš3yy ⲉⲡϣⲉ عفش *ʿifish*, 'cockroach, or other unpleasant insect'

pd 'to run, or run away,' perhaps origin of ⲡⲱⲧ يفطّ *yufuṭṭ* 'to jump'

fty ϥⲱⲧⲉ فوطة *fūṭa*, 'towel'

m3y ⲙⲟⲓ, 'lion'

my wnm ⲙⲁⲩⲱⲙ, 'give to eat'; مم *mam*, 'eat'

mw ⲙⲟⲟⲩ امبو *umbū* 'water'

mwt ⲘⲀⲀⲨ, 'mother'

mnỉ ⲚⲎⲚⲒ, 'honey pot,' origin of Arabic ناني *nāni*, 'honeycomb'

t3 mrỉ ⲦⲈⲘⲈⲢⲈ دميرة *dimīra*, 'land of reeds'

mrsw ⲘⲢⲒⲤ مريسة *marīsa*, a kind of Egyptian beer

mḫ3 ⲀⲘϢⲈ أمشة *amsha*, 'whip'

mḫyr ⲘϢⲒⲢ امشير *Amshīr* (month)

msw rʿ ⲘⲈⲤⲰⲢⲎ مسرى *Misra* (month)

mstpt 'box,' origin of مصطبة *maṣṭaba*, a crude brick seat

mḳr, 'vessel,' perhaps related to ⲘⲀⲔⲢⲞ مجور *majūr*, a type of mortar

n3 ʿn.s ⲚⲀⲚⲞⲨⲤ ننوس *nannūs*, 'she is beautiful' (a pet name)

nʿr, 'catfish'

nb ⲚⲞⲨⲂ, 'gold,' used in Arabic expression هوب هوب ياشغل النوب *hōb, hōb, ya shughl al-nōb*, 'Work, work! Work is gold!'; also found in Arabic as نبأ *nabaʾ*, 'gold'

nbỉt نبوت *nabbūt*, 'rod'

npry ⲚⲀⲠⲢⲈ نباري *nabāri*, 'grain'

nf ⲚⲒϤⲒ ينف *naff*, 'to blow one's nose'

nfrt نفرت *Nufret*, 'the beautiful one' (ancient woman's name revived for modern use) *nfrt.iry* نفرتاري *Nefertari*, 'their beautiful one' (ancient woman's name revived for modern use)

nfrt iti نفرتيتي *Nefertiti*, 'the beautiful one has come' (ancient woman's name revived for modern use)

nni ⲚⲞⲨⲚⲈ(ⲞⲨ) نونو *nūnu*, 'child or infant'

nrt ⲚⲞⲨⲢⲈ, 'vulture,' origin of Arabic نوري *nūri*, 'a rapacious imposter'

nḥb.f ⲚⲀϩⲂⲈϥ ناف *nāf*, 'yoke'

nsḳ ⲖⲰⲔⲤ لكش *lakash*, 'to attack'

☉ *rʿ*, 'sun'

rʿ-ms-sw, 'Ramesses' (name of a pharaoh)

rwš, 'to care,' perhaps with the negative *iwty* the source of the Arabic أطرش *aṭrash*, 'deaf'

rmw ⲢⲀⲘⲒ, 'fish,' origin of رمروم *ramrūm*, 'tilapia'

ršw ⲢⲀϢⲈ روشة *rawsha*, 'joy, gladness'

rsy ⲢⲎⲤ مريسي *marīsi*, 'south wind'

rḳʿ ⲢⲒⲔⲈ الرَك *al-rakk*, 'inclination'

rḳʿ ⲖⲀⲔϩ, 'corner,' origin of متلقح *mitlaqqaḥ*, 'neglected'

rdit ʿr, 'to cause to ascend,' origin of ⲦⲀⲖⲞ تلّ *tall*, 'to carry' *r dyt iry*, 'cause to do (something),' origin of ⲉⲑⲣⲉ أتاري *atāri*, 'this is why'

h3b ϩⲱⲃ, 'work,' used in Arabic expression هوب هوب ياشغل النوب *hōb, hōb, ya shughl al-nōb*, 'Work, work! Work is gold!'

h3nw ϩⲟⲉⲓⲙ, 'wave'; origin of ياحومتي *ya ḥōmti* 'oh my trouble!'

hb ϩⲃⲃⲉ حبأ *ḥaba'*, 'plow'

hbhb ϩⲟⲡϩⲉⲡ, 'tread, trample,' found in Arabic expression حبا حبا مين يجيني *ḥaba, ḥaba, mīn yigīni*, 'Walk, walk, who's coming to me?' (said to babies learning to walk); the Egyptian word is also the source of ϩⲟⲡϩⲡ هبهبه habhaba, 'fury and disturbance'

(with variant pronunciation of preceding) *hmhm* ϩⲟⲙϩⲉⲙ يحمحم *yiḥamḥam* 'to go around'

hnhn ϩⲗⲟⲟⲗⲉ هنّن hannin, 'to lull'

hrw, 'day'

ḥwš (Demotic), 'cursed,' origin of ϩⲟⲟⲩϣ حَوش *ḥawash*, 'hated people, unruly mob'

ḥb ϩⲟⲡ, 'feast'; cf.

ḥbs ϩⲱⲃⲥ حبايص *ḥabāyis*, 'clothes'

ḥpt ϩⲟⲡⲧ عبّط *'abbaṭ*, 'to embrace'

ḥmḏ ϩⲙϫ حامض *ḥāmiḍ*, 'vinegar'

ḥnw ϩⲛⲁⲩ حله *ḥalla*, a metal cooking pot shaped a little like a wok

ḥry ϩⲟⲓⲣⲉ, 'dung'; origin of هرّ harr, 'to have diarrhea'

ḥsy ϩⲱⲥ هوسة hawsa, 'to sing'

ḥt ḥr ϩⲁⲧⲱⲣ هاتور *Hatūr* (month)

ḥdb ϩⲧⲟⲡ طبّ *ṭabb*, 'to fall'

ḫ3rw ϩⲓⲣ حارة *ḥāra*, 'lane'

ḫbḫb ϣⲟⲃϣⲉⲃ شبشبة *shabshaba*, a kind of spell

ḫnfw ⲕⲉⲛⲉⲫⲓⲧⲉⲛ, possibly the Egyptian كنافة *kunāfa*, a kind of sweet pastry

ḫnft ϫⲛⲟϥ شنف *shinf*, 'basket'

ḫrp n msy ϣⲟⲣⲡ, cf. ϣⲟⲣⲡ ⲙ̄ⲙⲓⲥⲓ, 'first-born'; شرابي *Sharābi* (also Shirbi), 'first' (man's name)

ḫrs ϣⲣⲁϣ شرش *shirsh*, 'bundle'

ẖprt ϣⲡⲏⲣⲉ اشبار *ishbār*, 'miracle, amazing thing'

ẖnẖn, 'to scatter,' perhaps origin of ϩⲟⲗϩⲗ مهلهل *mihalhil*, 'in tatters'

ẖrt ϩⲣⲉⲩⲉ هروة *hiriuwa*, 'food'

ẖsy ϩⲓⲥⲉ هيصة *hēṣa*, 'trouble'

and

swnt ⲤⲞⲨⲀⲚ, 'trade'; اسوان *Aswān* (a city in Upper Egypt)

swḥt ⲤⲞⲞⲨϨⲈ سويحة *Swēḥa*, 'egg' (man's name)

spt ⲤⲠⲀϯ سُباطة *subāṭa*, 'cluster'

snw سنّ *sinn*, a kind of brown bread

snt ⲤⲰⲚⲈ 'sister,' سونة *Sūna*, a woman's nick-name

sẖ ⲤⲰϢ سخّة *sakhkha*, 'a light beating'

sẖn ϢⲀϢⲚⲒ, 'examine, look for,' ششني *shishni*, 'sample'

sšn ϢⲰϢⲈⲚ, 'lily' or 'lotus,' سوسن *Sawsan*, a woman's name (Susan)

sšd ϢⲞⲨϢⲦ شيش *shīsh*, 'shuttered windows'

st ستّ *sitt*, 'woman'

stf ⲤⲰⲦϤ شطف *shaṭaf*, 'to rinse'

š3wḳr ϢⲞⲨⲔⲢⲈ شكوريا *shakūrya*, 'greens'

š3š3 'twisted,' origin of ϢⲰϢ مشوّش *mishawwish*, 'confused of mind'

šꜥd ϢⲰⲰⲦ شوطة *shōṭa*, 'massacre, catastrophe, epidemic'

(later written as) *špst* ϢⲀⲠϢⲒ شوبش *shōbash*, 'distinguished, noble women'

šfyt ϢⲂⲎ شبيك *shubbēk*, 'your excellency'

šny ϢⲒⲚⲈ, 'inquiry,' used in expression شنّه ورنّه *shanna wa-ranna*, 'an inquiry and a ringing'

šnwt ϢⲈⲨⲚⲈ شونة *shōna*, 'granary'

šnḏt ϢⲞⲚⲦⲈ سنط *sanṭ*, 'acacia tree'

šrr, 'to be little'; with *k3*, 'nourishment,' source for ϢⲀⲢⲔⲈ شراقي *sharāqi*, 'dry, thirsty (land)'

šhb ϢⲰⲂϨ مشبوح *mashbūḥ*, 'scorched,' and ϢⲞϨⲂ شوب *shōb*, 'hot weather'

škr ϢⲔⲒⲖ شكارة *shikāra*, 'big sack'

𓈎

ḳ3b ⲔⲰⲂ, 'doubling,' origin of كبّب *kabbib*, 'accumulating (responsibilities)'

or *krṯ* ⲔⲈⲖⲖⲞϪ, 'puppy,' قلتة *Qulta*, a man's name

ḳrṯt (Demotic) ⲔⲈⲢⲎⲦ كرتة *karta*, 'remains of a meal'

ḳny ⲔⲎⲚⲈ, 'fat,' used in Arabic كاني وماني *kāni wa-māni* to express harmony

ḳnḳn perhaps origin of ϬⲚϬⲚ دندن *dandin*, 'to sing a song'

ḳrst ⲔⲀⲒⲤⲈ ياكاسي *ya kāsi* 'oh my burial!'

𓎡

kʿk ⲔⲀⲀⲔⲈ كعك *kaʿk*, an Egyptian cookie

k3 ḥr k3 ⲔⲞⲒⲀϨⲔ كيهك *Kiyahk* (month)

k3k3wt, perhaps related to ⲕⲉⲗⲕⲟⲩⲗⲉ or ⲕⲗⲕⲁ كلكوعة *kalkūʿa*, 'a lump'

kršt ⲕⲩⲗⲗⲏϭⲧⲓϩ جُلّاش *gullāsh*, a kind of savory pastry stuffed with meat or cheese

grb ϭⲟⲗⲃⲉ جلابية *jallabiya*, a man's overgarment

gḥs ϭϩⲟⲥ جحش *jaḥsh*, 'young donkey'

t3 ʿb ⲧⲱⲃⲉ طوبة *Ṭūba* (month)

t3w ϫⲓ, 'take,' found in Arabic expression شيكا بيكا *shīka-bīka!* 'Finish (your work)! Take your salary!'

titi ϯϯ تاتا *tāta*, 'tread, pace'

twt ⲧⲟⲟⲩⲧⲉ, 'to gather or collect,' used in Arabic expression توت حاوي *tūt ḥāwi!* 'gather round for the charmer!'

tbipsi (Demotic) ⲧⲉⲣⲡⲟⲥⲉ, 'baked brick,' origin of طربش *ṭurubsh*, 'stupid or dull person' and ترباس *tirbās*, 'person of dubious character, conspirator'

tbs ⲧⲱⲃⲥ, 'to prick,' origin of دبّوس *dabbūs*, 'a pin'

tftf ⲑⲟϥⲧⲉϥ تفتف *taftif*, 'to spit'

tms, 'buried,' origin of ⲧⲱⲙⲥ مدّمس *midammis*, beans cooked slowly in a covered pot *tr* ⲦⲰⲢⲈ طورية *ṭūrya*, 'hoe'

ṯḫ ϮϨⲈ or ⲐⲒϦⲒ طينة (*sakrān*) *ṭīna*, 'senselessly drunk'

ṯḫṯḫ ⲦⲀϨⲦϨ تهته *tahtih*, 'to be confused'

ṯ3b ϪⲞⲠ شُبّ *shubb*, 'big cup'

ṯbṯbt طبطب *ṭabṭab*, 'to pat someone's back in gesture of affection'

dy.t.ulʿ (Demotic) ⲐⲞⲨⲈⲖⲞ (or ⲦⲞⲨⲖⲞ) تِوِل *tiwil*, 'to confuse'

dbt ⲦⲰⲂⲈ طوبة *ṭūba*, a mud brick

dpt, 'ship'; possibly related to ذهبية *dahabiya*, a kind of Nile houseboat

dit inw ⲦⲚⲚⲞ̇ⲞⲨ, 'cause that they bring'; تنّه *tannuh*, 'cause to go' or 'start'

dšr, 'to be red (with anger?), perhaps origin of ⲦⲰⲢϢ, used in expression ايد طرشة *īd ṭursha*, 'heavy-handed blows'

ḏ3yt شاية *shāya*, 'shirt'

ḏ3ḏ3 ϪⲒϪⲰⲒ, 'head'; origin of شوشة *shūsha*, 'hair'

ḏpḥ, possibly source for ϪⲘⲠⲈϨ, var. ϪⲠⲞϨ تفّاح *tuffāḥ*, 'apples'

 *dfḏf* ϫⲟϥϫϥ مزفزف *mizafzif*, 'overheated'

 *ḏrt* ⲧⲣⲉ درّة *durra*, 'kite'

 *ḏḥwt* ⲑⲟⲟⲩⲧ توت *Tūt* (month)

ḏẖm (Demotic), 'sooty,' ϭⲱϧⲙ (or ϫⲱϩⲙ) سخّم *sakhkham*, 'to defile'

ḏḳ (Demotic) ϫⲱⲕ, 'finish,' found in Arabic expression شيكا بيكا *shīka-bīka!* 'Finish (your work)! Take your salary!'

ḏḳʿ (Demotic) ϫⲟⲕϫⲕ زقزق *zaqzaq*, 'to tickle or tease'

(L)

lbs (Demotic) ⲗⲟⲃⲥ لبيس *labīs*, a kind of Nile fish

Coptic

Note: Entries in this glossary are ordered alphabetically, not by root. In some cases the definite article ⲡ(ⲉ), ⲧ(ⲉ) or ⲛ(ⲉ) is appended to the entry because it was borrowed into Arabic with the article included.

ⲁ

ⲁⲃⲥⲱⲛ, 'mint,' *ỉbsꜣ*, perhaps origin of ايسون *aysūn*, a kind of anise drink

ⲁϥ *ꜥf* عفّ *ꜥaff*, 'fly'

ⲁⲕⲱ *ꜣḳ* عك *ꜥakk,* 'to destroy'

ⲁⲗⲟⲩ *ꜥlw* (Demotic), 'child, boy,' used in expression ياعيّل *yaꜥayyil!* and its contracted from *y-ala!* 'hey, young man!'

ⲁⲙⲛⲧⲉ *ỉmntt* امندي *amendi,* 'hell, the underworld'

ⲁⲙϣⲉ *mḫꜣ* أمشة *amsha,* 'whip'

ⲁⲛ *ꜥn* عاد *ꜥād*, superfluous particle in a negative sentence

Ⲃ

ⲂⲈⲈⲂⲈ  *b3b3i* بأبأ *ba'ba'*, 'to bubble up'; and بعبع *ba'ba'*, 'to boil'

ⲂⲈⲔⲈ  *b3k* 'salary; work,' found in the expression شيكا بيكا *shīka-bīka!* 'Finish your work if you want to get paid!'

ⲂⲒⲢⲤⲒⲘ  *brsm* برسيم *barsīm*, 'clover'

ⲂⲒⲤⲀ  *b3stt* بيسا *Bīsa,* 'the goddess Bastet' (woman's name)

ⲂⲚⲚⲈ  *bnri* بِنّي *binni*, 'dates'

ⲂⲞϬⲤ  *bgs* بوّج *bawwij*, 'to rebel'

ⲂⲰⲢⲈ  *br* بوري *būri*, 'mullet'

Ⲉ

ⲈⲐⲢⲈ أتاري *atāri*, 'this is why,' from  *rdyt iry*, 'cause to do (something)'

ⲈⲒⲈϨ ⲈⲖⲞⲞⲖ,  *3ḥt i3rrt*, 'vineyard,' literally 'field of grapes'; found in expression ياحليلة ياحليلة *yaḥlēla, yaḥlēla*, 'how sweet, how sweet'

ⲈⲠⲎⲠ  *ipip* أبيب *Abīb* (month)

ⲈⲠϢⲈ  *pš3yy* عفش *'ifish*, 'cockroach or other unpleasant insect'

ⲈⲢⲦⲞⲂ اردب *ardab*, a unit of measure of dry weight

Ⲑ

ⲐⲒϧⲒ see ϯϨⲈ

ⲐⲞⲞⲨⲦ  *ḏḥw.t* توت *Tūt* (month)

ⲐⲞⲨⲈⲖⲞ (or ⲦⲞⲨⲖⲞ) *dy.t.ul*ʿ (Demotic) تِوِل *tiwil*, 'to confuse'

ⲐⲞϤⲦⲈϤ *tftf* تفتف *taftif*, 'to spit'

I

ⲒⲞⲘ *ym* يم *yamm*, 'sea'

ⲒⲞϨ *iʿḥ*, 'moon'; found in Coptic expression ⲞⲨⲰϨ ⲞⲨⲰϨ ⲒⲞϨ and equivalent Arabic expression وحوي ياوحوي ايوحة *waḥawy ya waḥawy iyūḥa* 'welcome, welcome, o crescent'

K

ⲔⲀⲀⲔⲈ *kʿk* كعك *kaʿk*, an Egyptian cookie

ⲔⲀⲒⲤⲈ *ḳrst* ياكاسي *ya kāsi*, 'oh my burial!'

ⲔⲈⲚⲈⲪⲒⲦⲈⲚ *ẖnfw*, possibly the Egyptian كنافة *kunāfa*, a kind of sweet pastry

ⲔⲈⲖⲖⲞϪ or *krṯ* قلتة *Qulta*, a man's name originally meaning 'puppy'

ⲔⲈⲖⲔⲞⲨⲖⲈ or ⲔⲖⲔⲀ كلكوعة *kalkūʿa*, 'a lump,' perhaps related to *k3k3wt*

ⲔⲈⲢⲎⲦ *ḳrṯt* (Demotic) كرتة *karta*, 'remains of a meal'

ⲔⲎⲚⲈ *ḳny*, 'fat,' used in Arabic كاني وماني *kānī wa-mānī* to express harmony

ⲔⲞⲒⲀϨⲔ *k3 ḥr k3* كيهك *Kiyahk* (month)

ⲔⲞⲨⲔⲖⲀ from Greek κουκούλλιον, 'a hood or cowl of monks,' origin of كاكولة *kakūla*, 'long overcoat'

ⲔⲢⲞⲨϪ 'a disk or something round,' origin of قرص *qurṣ,* a round, baked or fried cake

ⲔⲨⲖⲖⲎϬⲦⲒϨ *kršt* جُلاّش *gullāsh*, a kind of savory pastry stuffed with meat or cheese

ⲔⲰⲂ *ḳ3b*, 'doubling,' origin of كبّب *kabbib*, 'to accumulate'

Ⲗ

ⲖⲀⲔϨ *rḳ*ʿ, 'corner,' origin of متلقح *mitlaqqaḥ*, 'neglected'

ⲖⲀⲠⲦ or ⲖⲀⲦⲠ لفت *lift*, 'salt turnip, pickled turnip'

ⲖⲞⲂⲤ *lbs* (Demotic) لبيس *labīs*, a kind of Nile fish

ⲖⲞⲨⲖⲀⲒ 'to shout (with joy),' origin of ياليل *ya lēl*, traditional introduction to many Egyptian songs

ⲖⲰⲔⲤ *nsḳ* لكش *lakash*, 'to attack'

Ⲙ

ⲘⲀⲀⲨ *mwt*, 'mother'

ⲘⲀⲔⲢⲞ مجور *majūr*, 'a type of mortar,' perhaps derived from *mḳr* 'vessel'

ⲘⲀⲢⲈ 'let (us go),' found as particle used in imperative expressions such as ماتشتغل *ma-tishtaghal!* 'get to work!'

ⲘⲀⲨⲰⲘ, 'food,' *my wnm*, 'give to eat,' مم *mam*, 'eat'

ⲘⲈⲤⲰⲢⲎ *msw r*ʿ مسرى *Misra* (month)

ⲘⲈϢⲈ *bw rḫ* مش *mish*, 'not'

ⲘⲞⲈⲒⲦ ميت *mīt,* 'way,' used in compound place names, such as *Mīt Ghamr* and *Mīt Abu al-Kom*

ⲘⲞⲒ *m3y*, 'lion'

ⲘⲞⲞⲨ *mw* امبو *umbū,* 'water'

ⲘⲢⲒⲤ *mrsw* مريسة *marīsa,* a kind of Egyptian beer

ⲘϢⲒⲢ *mḫyr* امشير *Amshīr* (month)

N

ⲚⲀⲚⲞⲨⲤ *n3 ʿn.s* ننوس *nannūs*, 'she is beautiful' (a pet name)

ⲚⲀⲠⲢⲈ *npry* نباري *nabāri,* 'grain'

ⲚⲀϨⲂⲈϤ *nḥb.f* ناف *nāf,* 'yoke'

ⲚⲎⲚⲒ *mni*, 'honey pot,' origin of Arabic ناني *nāni,* 'honeycomb'

ⲚⲒϤⲒ *nf* نف *naff,* 'to blow one's nose'

ⲚⲞⲨⲂ *nb*,. 'gold,' used in the expression هوب هوب ياشغل النوب *hōb, hōb, ya shughl al-nōb,* 'Work, work! Work is gold!'; also found in Arabic as نبأ *naba'*, 'gold'

ⲚⲞⲨⲚⲈ(ⲞⲨ) *nni* نونو *nūnu,* 'child or infant'

ⲚⲞⲨⲢⲈ *nrt*, 'vulture,' origin of Arabic نوري *nūri*, 'a rapacious imposter'

O

ⲞⲒⲠⲈ *ipt* ويبة *wēba*, a unit of measurement of dry weight

ⲞⲨⲀϨⲂⲈϤ *wḥwḥ* يوحوح *yiwaḥwaḥ*, 'to groan'
ⲞⲨⲰϨ *w3ḥ*, 'to stay, put'; used in Coptic expression ⲞⲨⲰϨ ⲞⲨⲰϨ ⲒⲞϨ and equivalent Arabic expression وحوي ياوحوي ايوحة *waḥawy ya waḥawy iyūḥa* 'welcome, welcome, o crescent'
ⲞⲨϪⲀⲒ *wḏ3* جاي *jāy*, 'cry out from pain for rescue'

Ⲡ

ⲠⲀⲚⲞⲨⲠ *p3 inpw* بانوب *Banūb*, 'he who belongs to the god Anubis' (man's name)
ⲠⲀⲞⲠⲈ *p3 (n) ipt* بابه *Bāba* (month)
ⲠⲀⲢⲘⲞⲨⲦϨ *p3 n rnnt* برمودة *Barmūda* (month)
ⲠⲀⲢⲘϨⲞⲦⲠ *p3 n imn-ḥtpw* برمهات *Baramhāt* (month)
ⲠⲀⲦⲀⲨ *p3tw* بَتّاو *battāw*, a kind of bread
ⲠⲀⲰⲚⲈ *p3 (n) int* بؤونة *Ba'ūna* (month)
ⲠⲀϢⲞⲚⲤ *p3 n ḫnsw* بشنس *Bashans* (month)
ⲠⲀϨⲞⲢ *p3 n ḥr* باهور *Bahūr*, 'he who belongs to Horus' (man's name)
ⲠⲀϦⲰⲘ *p3 ꜥḫm* باخوم *Bakhūm*, 'god's image' (man's name)
ⲠⲒⲰⲘ *p3 (n) ym* بيومي *Bayūmi*, 'he of the river or sea' (man's name)
ⲠⲒϦ *p3 3ḫ* بخ *bikh*, 'demon'
ⲠⲔⲞⲦ *p3 ḳd* بقوطي *baqūṭi*, 'small basket'

ⲠⲞⲨⲰϢ *pꜣ wḫꜣ* بوش *bōsh*, 'dream, desire'

ⲠⲤⲀⲦⲈ *pꜣ sṯt* بساده *Bisāda*, 'the light' (man's name)

ⲠⲰⲢϢ and *prḫ* برش *bursh*, 'mat'

ⲠⲰⲦ يفطّ *yufuṭṭ*, 'to jump,' perhaps derived from *pd*, 'to run, or run away'

ⲠⲰϨ *pḥ* بَح *baḥḥ*, 'to come to an end'

ⲠϢⲞⲒ *pꜣ šꜣi* بشاي *Bishāy*, 'fate, destiny' (man's name)

ⲠϢⲰϢ *pꜣ ḫꜣḫꜣ* فشوش *fashūsh*, 'failure'

Ⲣ

ⲢⲀⲘⲒ *rmw*, 'fish,' origin of رمروم *ramrūm*, 'tilapia'

ⲢⲀϢⲈ *ršw* روشة *rawsha*, 'joy, gladness'

ⲢⲎⲒ راي *rāy*, a kind of fish

ⲢⲎⲤ *rsy* مريسي *marīsī* 'south wind'

ⲢⲒⲔⲈ *rkꜥ*, 'inclination,' الرَك *al-rakk*, 'it depends'

Ⲥ

ⲤⲀⲘⲒⲦ from Greek σεμίδαλις, 'flour,' origin of سميط *samīṭ*, a bread made of fine white flour

ⲤⲒⲘⲤⲒⲘ سمسم *simsim*, 'sesame'

ⲤⲞⲞⲨϨⲈ *swḥt* سويحة *Swēḥa*, 'egg' (man's name)

ⲤⲞⲨⲀⲚ *swnt*, 'trade'; اسوان *Aswān* (a city in Upper Egypt)

ⲤⲠⲀϮ *spt* سُباطة *subāṭa,* 'cluster'

ⲤⲰⲚⲈ *snt*, 'sister,' سونة *Sūna*, a woman's nick-name

ⲤⲰⲦϤ *stf* شطف *shaṭaf,* 'rinsed'

ⲤⲰϢ *sḫ* سخّة *sakhkha*, 'a light beating'

T

ⲦⲀⲖⲞ, 'to carry,' derived from *rdit ʿr*, 'to cause to ascend'; تلّ *tall*, 'to carry'

ⲦⲀϨⲦϨ *tḫtḫ* تهته *tahtih*, 'to be confused'

ⲦⲈⲒⲈⲂⲦ, 'eastern,' *tꜣ iꜣb.ty*; تياب *tiyāb*, 'east wind'

ⲦⲈⲘⲈⲢⲈ *tꜣ mri*, 'land of reeds,' دميرة *dimīra*, 'flood season'

ⲦⲈⲠⲰ *ṯꜣ pꜣyt* ضبّة *ḍabba,* part of the fastening of a door

ⲦⲈⲢⲠⲞⲤⲈ *tbipsi* (Demotic), 'baked brick,' origin of طربش *ṭurubsh*, 'stupid or dull person,' and ترباس *tirbās*, 'person of dubious character, conspirator'

ⲦⲚⲚⲞⲞⲨ *dit inw*, 'cause that they bring'; تنّه *tannuh*, 'cause to go' or 'start'

ⲦⲞⲞⲨⲦⲈ *twt*, 'to gather or collect,' used in the expression توت حاوي *tūt ḥāwi!* 'gather round for the charmer!'

ⲦⲞⲨⲖⲞ see ⲐⲞⲨⲈⲖⲞ

ⲦⲢⲈ *ḏrt* درّة *durra*, 'kite'

ⲦⲰⲂⲈ *dbt* طوبة *ṭūba,* 'mud brick'

ⲦⲰⲂⲈ *tꜣ ꜥb* طوبة *Ṭūba* (month)

ⲦⲰⲂⲤ *tbs*, 'to prick,' origin of دبّوس *dabbūs*, 'a pin'

ⲦⲰⲘⲤ مدّمس *midammis*, a method of cooking beans slowly in a pot, derived from *tms*, 'buried'

ⲦⲰⲢⲈ *tr* طورية *ṭūrya*, 'hoe'

ⲦⲰⲢϢ, used in expression ايد طرشة *īd ṭursha*, 'heavy-handed blows,' perhaps derived from *dšr*, 'to be red (with anger?)'

ⲫ

ⲫⲈⲖ *pr* فول *fūl*, 'fava beans'

ⲫⲖⲎⲞⲨ or ⲈⲠⲢⲀ فهلوه *fahlawa*, 'deceit' perhaps derived from *prt* 'vanities'

ⲱ

ⲰⲚⲈ *inr* 'rock'

ⲰⲚⲈ *int*, 'valley'

ⲰϪⲚ *ꜥḏn* (Demotic), 'to destroy,' origin of اجنة *ajana*, 'iron chisel'

ϣ

ϢⲀⲠϢⲒ *špst* شوبش *shōbash*, 'distinguished, noble women'

ϢⲀⲢⲔⲈ شراقي *sharāqi*, 'dry, thirsty land,' derived from *šrr*, 'to be little,' and *kꜣ*, 'nourishment' ϣⲁϣⲛⲓ *sẖn*, 'examine, look for,' ششني *shishni*, 'sample'

ϣⲃⲏ *šfyt* شبيك *shubbēk*, 'your excellency'

ϣⲉⲛⲟⲩⲧⲉ *ʿnḫ nṯr* شنودة *Shenūda*, 'God lives' (man's name)

ϣⲉⲩⲛⲉ *šnwt* شونة *shōna*, 'granary'

ϣⲓⲛⲉ *šny*, 'inquiry,' used in expression شنّه ورنه *shanna wa-ranna*, 'inquiry and a ringing'

ϣⲕⲓⲗ *škr* شكارة *shikāra*, 'big sack'

ϣⲟⲃϣⲉⲃ *ḫbḫb* شبشبة *shabshaba*, a kind of spell

ϣⲟⲗϣⲗ شلشل *shalshal*, 'to pull violently on something'

ϣⲟⲛⲧⲉ *šnḏt* سنط *sanṭ*, 'acacia tree'

ϣⲟⲣⲡ, cf. ϣⲟⲣⲡ ⲙ̄ⲙⲓⲥⲓ *ẖrp n msy*, 'first-born'; شرابي *Sharābi* (also Shirbi), 'first' (man's name)

ϣⲟⲩⲕⲣⲉ *š3wḳr* شكوريا *shakūrya*, 'greens'

ϣⲟⲩϣⲧ *sšd* شيش *shīsh*, 'shuttered windows'

ϣⲡⲏⲣⲉ *ẖprt* اشبار *ishbār*, 'miracle, amazing thing'

ϣⲣⲁϣ *ḫrs* شرش *shirsh*, 'bundle'

ϣⲱⲱⲧ *šʿd* شوطة *shōṭa*, 'massacre, catastrophe, epidemic'

ϣⲱⲃϩ *šhb* مشبوح *mashbūḥ*, 'scorched,' and ϣⲟϩⲃ شوب *shōb*, 'hot weather' ϣⲱϣ مشوّش *mishawwish*, 'confused of mind,' derived from *š3š3* 'twisted'

ϣⲱϣⲉⲛ *sšn*, 'lily' or 'lotus,' سوسن *Sawsan*, a woman's name (Susan)

ϥ

ϥⲣϥⲉⲣ *brbr* يفرفر *yifarfar*, 'to shake, shiver'

ϥⲱⲧⲉ *fṯy* فوطة *fūṭa*, 'towel'

ϩ

ϩⲁⲗⲱⲙ حلوم *ḥalūm*, 'cheese'

ϩⲁⲙⲉ, 'temperament,' used in the expression شاف خيمه *shāf khīmuh*, 'to study his temperament'

ϩⲁⲧⲱⲣ *ḥt ḥr* هاتور *Hatūr* (month)

ϩⲃⲃⲉ *hb* حبأ *ḥaba'*, 'plow'

ϩⲓⲣ *ḫ3rw* حارة *ḥāra*, 'lane'

ϩⲓⲥⲉ *ẖsy* هيصة *hēṣa*, 'trouble'

ϩⲗⲟⲟⲗⲉ *hnhn* هنّن *hannin*, 'to lull'

ϩⲙϫ *ḥmḏ* حامض *ḥāmiḍ*, 'vinegar'

ϩⲛⲁⲩ *ḥnw* حله *ḥalla*, a metal cooking pot shaped a little like a wok

ϩⲟⲉⲓⲙ *h3nw*, 'wave'; origin of ياحومتي *ya ḥōmti*, 'oh my trouble!'

ϩⲟⲓⲣⲉ *ḥry* 'dung'; origin of هرّ *harr*, 'to have diarrhea'

ϩⲟⲗϩⲗ مهلهل *mihalhil*, 'in tatters,' perhaps derived from *ẖnẖn*, 'to scatter'

ϨⲞⲘϨⲈⲘ *hmhm* يحمحم *yiḥamḥam,* 'to go around'

ϨⲞⲞⲨϢ حَوش *ḥawash,* 'hated people, unruly mob,' derived from *ḥwš* (Demotic) 'cursed'

ϨⲞⲠϨⲈⲠ *hbhb*, 'tread, trample,' found in the expression حبا حبا مين يجيني *ḥaba, ḥaba, mīn yigīni,* 'Walk, walk, who's coming to me?' (said to babies learning to walk); the Egyptian word is also the source of ϨⲞⲠϨⲠ هبهبه *habhaba,* 'fury and disturbance'

ϨⲞⲠ *ḥb*, 'feast'

ϨⲞⲠⲦ *ḥpt* عبّط *ʿabbaṭ,* 'to embrace'

ϨⲢⲈⲨⲈ *ẖrt* هروة *hiriwwa,* 'food'

ϨⲦⲞⲠ *ḥdb* طبّ *ṭabb,* 'to fall'

ϨⲰⲂ *h3b*, 'work,' used in the expression هوب هوب ياشغل النوب *hōb, hōb, ya shughl al-nōb,* 'Work, work! Work is gold!'

ϨⲰⲂⲤ *ḥbs* حبايص *ḥabāyis,* 'clothes'

ϨⲰⲤ *ḥsy* هوسة *hawsa,* 'to sing'

Ϫ

ϪⲈⲔϪⲒⲔ زقازيق *zaqazīq,* 'small fish'

ϪⲈⲘϪⲞⲘ, 'strong,' origin of جمجوم *Jamjūm* (also pronounced *Gamgūm*), man's name

ϪⲒ *t3w*, 'take,' found in the expression شيكا بيكا *shīka-bīka!* 'Finish (your work)! Take your salary!'

ϫⲓⲣ صير *ṣīr,* a kind of small fish, eaten with salt and taken as a metaphor for extremely salty food

ϫⲓϫⲱⲓ *ḏ3ḏ3*, 'head'; origin of شوشة *shūsha*, 'hair'

ϫⲙⲡⲉϩ, var. ϫⲡⲟϩ تفّاح *tuffāḥ* 'apples,' possibly derived from *ḏpḥ*

ϫⲛⲟϥ *ḫnft* شنف *shinf*, 'basket'

ϫⲟⲡ *ṯ3b* شُبّ *shubb*, 'big cup'

ϫⲟϥϫϥ *ḏfḏf* مزفزف *mizafzif*, 'overheated'

ϫⲡⲟϩ see ϫⲙⲡⲉϩ

ϫⲱⲕ *ḏk* (Demotic) 'finish,' found in the expression شيكا بيكا *shīka-bīka!* 'Finish (your work)! Take your salary!'

ϫⲟ ⲕⲥⲓ or ϭⲁⲧⲥⲉ جيّص *jayyaṣ*, 'break wind'

ϫⲟⲕϫⲕ *ḏkʿ* (Demotic) زقزق *zaqzaq*, 'to tickle or tease'

ϫⲱϩⲙ see ϭⲱϧⲙ

ϭ

ϭⲁⲧⲥⲉ see ϫⲟⲕⲥⲓ

ϭⲏⲗ جلجل *jiljil*, 'a small rattle or bell'

ϭⲛϭⲛ دندن *dandin*, 'to sing a song,' perhaps derived from *ḳnḳn*

ϭⲗⲃⲟⲟⲩ شلبة *shilba*, a kind of fish

ϭⲗⲟⲓ or ϭⲱⲗ, 'ball,' now applied only to the ball used in shot-put, جلّة *julla*

ϭⲟⲗⲃⲉ *grb* جلابية *jallabiya*, a man's overgarment

ϭωϧⲙ (or ϫⲱϩⲙ) *d̲ḫm* (Demotic), 'sooty,' سخّم *sakhkham*, 'to defile'

ϭϩⲟⲥ *gḥs* جحش *jaḥsh,* 'young donkey'

ϯ

ϯⲙⲉ, 'town,' commonly used in Egyptian place names, such as طما *Ṭima*, طماي *Ṭamāy*, and تميّ *Timayy*

ϯϯ *titi* تاتا *tāta*, 'tread, pace'

ϯϩⲉ or ⲑⲓϧⲓ *tḫ* طينة (*sakrān*) *ṭīna*, 'senselessly (drunk)'

Arabic

أ

أبيب *Abīb* *ipip* ⲈⲠⲎⲠ (month)

أتاري *atāri* ⲈⲐⲢⲈ, 'this is why,' from *r dyt iry*, 'cause to do (something)'

اجنة *ajana*, 'iron chisel,' derived from *ʿḏn* (Demotic) ⲰϪⲚ 'to destroy'

اسوان *Aswān* (a city in Upper Egypt), from *swnt* ⲤⲞⲨⲀⲚ, 'trade'

اشبار *ishbār* ϢⲠⲎⲢⲈ *ḫprt*, 'miracle, amazing thing'

أطرش *aṭrash*, 'deaf,' perhaps derived from *iwty*, a negative pronoun, with *rwš*, 'to care'

أكل العيش *akl al-ʿaysh* 'to eat bread,' a metaphor for earning one's living; cf. Egyptian *wnm t*

امبو *umbū* *mw* ⲘⲞⲞⲨ, 'water'

أمشة *amsha* *mḫ3* ⲀⲘϢⲈ, 'whip'

امندي *amendi* *imntt* ⲀⲘⲚⲦⲈ, 'hell, the underworld'

امشير *Amshīr* *mḫyr* ⲘϢⲒⲢ (month)
ايسون *aysūn,* a kind of anise drink, perhaps derived from *ibsꜣ* ⲀⲂⲤⲰⲚ, 'mint'
إيزيس *Izis* *ist*, 'Isis' (ancient goddess; revived as woman's name)
آه *ah!* (or أيوه , *aywa!*) *ꜣ*, 'yes'

ب

بأبأ *baʾbaʾ* 'to bubble up' and بعبع *baʿbaʿ*, 'to boil,' from *bꜣbꜣi* ⲂⲈⲈⲂⲈ
بابه *Bāba* *pꜣ* (*n*) *ipt* ⲠⲀⲞⲠⲈ (month)
بانوب *Bānūb* (man's name) *pꜣ inpw* ⲠⲀⲚⲞⲨⲠ, 'he who belongs to the god Anubis'
باهور *Bahūr* (man's name) *pꜣ n ḥr* ⲠⲀϨⲞⲢ, 'he who belongs to Horus'
ياباي *ya bāy*, from *bꜣ* 'soul, spirit'
بَتّاو *battāw* *pꜣtw* ⲠⲀⲦⲀⲨ, a kind of bread
بخ *bikh* *pꜣ ꜣḫ* ⲠⲒϧ, 'demon'
باخوم *Bakhūm* (man's name) *pꜣ ʿḥm* ⲠⲀϧⲰⲘ, 'god's image'
بَح *baḥḥ,* *pḥ* ⲠⲰϨ, 'to come to an end'
برسيم *barsim* *brsm* ⲂⲒⲢⲤⲒⲘ, 'clover'
برش *bursh* and *prḫ* ⲠⲰⲢϢ, 'mat'
برمهات *Barambāt* *pꜣ n imn-ḥtpw* ⲠⲀⲢⲘϨⲞⲦⲠ (month)
برمودة *Barmūda* *pꜣ n rnnt* ⲠⲀⲢⲘⲞⲨⲦϨ (month)

بساده *Bisāda* (man's name) *p3 sṯt* ⲠⲤⲀⲦⲈ, 'the light'

بشاي *Bishāy* (man's name) *p3 š3i* ⲠϢⲞⲒ, 'fate, destiny'

بشنس *Bashans* *p3 n ḫnsw* ⲠⲀϢⲞⲚⲤ (month)

بصاره *biṣāra*, a bean dish, perhaps from *ps-wr*, 'very cooked' or from , 'cooking,' and , *iwryt*, 'beans'

بطّيخ *baṭṭīkh* *bddk3*, 'watermelon'

بقوطي *baqūṭi* *p3 ḳd* ⲠⲔⲞⲦ, 'small basket'

بنّي *binni* *bnri* ⲂⲚⲚⲈ, 'dates'

بوّج *bawwij* *bgs* ⲂⲞϬⲤ, 'to rebel'

بوري *būri* *br* ⲂⲰⲢⲈ, 'mullet'

بوش *bōsh* *p3 wḫ3* ⲠⲞⲨⲰϢ, 'dream, desire'

بؤونة *Ba'ūna* *p3 (n) int* ⲠⲀⲰⲚⲈ (month)

بيسا *Bīsa* (woman's name) *b3stt* ⲂⲒⲤⲀ, 'the goddess Bastet'

بيكا *bīka* 'salary,' found in the expression شيكا بيكا *shīka-bīka!* 'Finish (your work)! Take your salary!' derived in part from *b3k* ⲂⲈⲔⲈ, 'salary, work'

بيومي *Bayūmi* (man's name) *p3 (n) ym* ⲠⲒⲰⲘ, 'he of the river or sea'

ت

تاتا *tāta* *titi* ⲦⲦ, 'tread, pace'

ترباس *tirbās*, 'person of dubious character, conspirator,' from *tbipsi* (Demotic) ⲦⲈⲢⲠⲞⲤⲈ, 'baked brick'

تفتف *taftif* *tftf* ⲑⲟϥⲧⲉϥ, 'to spit'

تفاح *tuffāḥ* ϫⲙⲡⲉϩ, var. ϫⲡⲟϩ, 'apples,' possibly from *ḏpḥ*

تلّ *tall* ⲧⲁⲗⲟ, 'to carry,' from *rdit ʿr*, 'to cause to ascend'

تنّه *tannuh* 'cause to go' or 'start,' from *dit inw* ⲧⲛⲛⲟⲟⲩ, 'cause that they bring'

تهته *tahtih* *tḫtḫ* ⲧⲁϩⲧϩ, 'to be confused'

توت *Tūt* *ḏḥwt* ⲑⲟⲟⲩⲧ (month)

توت *tūt*, used in the expression توت حاوي *tūt ḥāwi!* 'gather round for the charmer!' from *twt* ⲧⲟⲟⲩⲧⲉ, 'to gather or collect'

تِول *tiwil* *dy.t.ulʿ* (Demotic) ⲑⲟⲩⲉⲗⲟ (or ⲧⲟⲩⲗⲟ), 'to confuse'

تياب *tiyāb*, 'east wind,' from *ṯ3 i3b.ty* ⲧⲉⲓⲉⲃⲧ, 'eastern'

ج

جاي *jāy* *wḏ3* ⲟⲩϫⲁⲓ, 'cry out from pain for rescue'

جحش *jaḥsh* *gḥs* ϭϩⲟⲥ 'young donkey'

جلة *julla*, 'ball used in shot-put,' from ϭⲗⲟⲓ or ϭⲱⲗ, 'ball'

جلابية *jallabiya* *grb* ϭⲟⲗⲃⲉ, a man's overgarment

جلجل *jiljil* ϭⲏⲗ, small rattle or bell

جُلاش *gullāsh* *kršt* ⲕⲩⲗⲗⲏϭⲧⲓϩ, a kind of savory pastry stuffed with meat or cheese

جمجوم *Jamjūm* (also pronounced *Gamgūm*; man's name) from ϪⲈⲘϪⲞⲘ, 'strong'

جيّص *jayyaṣ* ϪⲞⲔⲤⲒ or ϬⲀⲦⲤⲈ, 'break wind'

ح

حارة *ḥāra* *ḫ3rw* ϨⲒⲢ, 'lane'

حبأ *ḥaba'* *hb* ϨⲂⲂⲈ, 'plow'

حبا *ḥaba*, used in the expression حبا حبا مين يجيني *ḥaba, ḥaba, mīn yigīni*, 'Walk, walk, who's coming to me?' (said to babies learning to walk), from *hbhb* ϨⲞⲠϨⲈⲠ, 'tread, trample'

هبهبه *habhaba* ϨⲞⲠϨⲠ, 'fury and disturbance,' from *hbhb*, 'tread, trample'

حبايص *ḥabāyis* *ḥbs* ϨⲰⲂⲤ, 'clothes'

حله *ḥalla* *ḥnw* ϨⲚⲀⲨ, a metal cooking pot shaped a little like a wok

حلوم *ḥalūm* ϨⲀⲖⲰⲘ, 'cheese'

حليلة *ḥalēla*, used in expression ياحليلة ياحليلة *ya ḥlēla, ya ḥlēla* 'how sweet, how sweet,' from *3ḥt i3rrt* ⲈⲒⲈϨ ⲈⲖⲞⲞⲖ, 'vineyard,' literally 'field of grapes'

يحمحم *yiḥamḥam* *hmhm* ϨⲞⲘϨⲈⲘ, 'to go around'

حامض *ḥāmiḍ* *ḥmḏ* ϨⲘϪ, 'vinegar'

حَوش *ḥawash* ϨⲞⲞⲨϢ, 'hated people, unruly mob,' from *ḥwš* (Demotic), 'cursed'

ياحومتي *ya-ḥōmti*, 'oh my trouble!' from *h3nw* ϨⲞⲈⲒⲘ, 'wave'

خ

خيم *khīm* 2ⲀⲘⲈ, 'temperament,' used in the expression شاف خيمه *shāf khīmuh,* 'to study his temperament'

د

دبّوس *dabbūs* 'a pin,' from *tbs* ⲦⲰⲂⲤ, 'to prick'

درّة *durra* *ḏrt* ⲦⲢⲈ, 'kite'

مدّمس *midammis* ⲦⲰⲘⲤ, a method of cooking beans slowly in a pot, from *tms* 'buried'

دميرة *dimīra,* 'flood season,' from *t3 mri*, 'land of reeds' ⲦⲈⲘⲈⲢⲈ

دندن *dandin* ϬⲚϬⲚ, 'to sing a song,' perhaps from *ḳnḳn*

ذهبية *dahabiya,* a kind of Nile houseboat, possibly from *dpt*, 'ship'

دوسة *Dōsa*, a woman's nickname, from *t3 ist,* the goddess Isis

ر

راي *rāy* ⲢⲎⲒ, a kind of fish

اردب *ardab* ⲈⲢⲦⲞⲂ, a unit of measure of dry weight

الرَك *al-rakk*, 'it depends' *rkʿ* ⲢⲒⲔⲈ, 'inclination'

رمروم *ramrūm*, 'tilapia,' from *rmw* ⲢⲀⲘⲒ, 'fish'

روشة *rawsha* *ršw* ⲢⲀϢⲈ, 'joy, gladness'

ز

زقزق *zaqzaq* *ḏḳ*ˁ (Demotic) ϫⲟⲕϫⲕ, 'to tickle or tease'

زقازيق *zaqazīq* ϫⲉⲕϫⲓⲕ, 'small fish'

مزفزف *mizafzif* *ḏfḏf* ϫⲟϥϫϥ, 'overheated'

س

سُباطة *subāṭa* *spt* ⲥⲡⲁϯ, 'cluster'

ستّ *sitt* *st*, 'woman'

سخّة *sakhkha* *sẖ* ⲥⲱϣ, 'a light beating'

سخّم *sakhkham*, 'to defile,' ϭⲱϧⲙ (or ϫⲱϩⲙ) from *ḏẖm* (Demotic), 'sooty'

سمسم *simsim* ⲥⲓⲙⲥⲓⲙ, 'sesame'

سميط *samīṭ* a bread made of fine white flour, from ⲥⲁⲙⲓⲧ, from Greek σεμίδαλις, 'flour'

سنّ *sinn* *snw*, a kind of brown bread

سنط *sanṭ* *šnḏt* ϣⲟⲛⲧⲉ, acacia tree

سوسن *Sawsan* *sšn* ϣⲱϣⲉⲛ, 'lily' or 'lotus,' a woman's name (Susan)

سونة *Sūna,* a woman's nickname, from ⲥⲱⲛⲉ *snt,* 'sister'

سويحة *Swēḥa,* a man's name, *swḥt* ⲥⲟⲟⲩϩⲉ, 'egg'

ش

شاية *shāya* *ḏ3yt*, 'shirt'

شُبّ *shubb* *ṯ3b* ϫⲟⲡ, 'big cup'

مشبوح *mashbūḥ* from *šhb* ϣⲱⲃϩ, 'scorched'

شبشبة *shabshaba* *ẖbẖb* ϣⲟⲃϣⲉⲃ, a kind of spell

شبيك *shubbēk* *šfyt* ϢⲂⲎ, 'your excellency'

شرابي *Sharābi* (also Shirbi), a man's name, from ϢⲞⲢⲠ, 'first'; cf. *ḫrp n msy* ϢⲞⲢⲠ Ⲙ̄ⲘⲒⲤⲒ 'first-born'

شرش *shirsh* *ḫrs* ϢⲢⲀϢ, 'bundle'

شراقي *sharāqi* ϢⲀⲢⲔⲈ, 'dry, thirsty land,' from *šrr*, 'to be little,' and *k3*, 'nourishment'

ششني *shishni*, 'sample' *sḫn* ϢⲀϢⲚⲒ, 'examine, look for'

شطف *shaṭaf* *stf* ⲤⲰⲦϤ, 'rinsed'

شكارة *shikāra* *škr* ϢⲔⲒⲖ, 'big sack'

شكوريا *shakūrya* *š3wḳr* ϢⲞⲨⲔⲢⲈ, 'greens'

شلبة *shilba* ϬⲖⲂⲞⲞⲨ, a kind of fish

شلشل *shalshal* ϢⲞⲖϢⲖ, 'to pull violently on something'

شنّة *shanna*, used in the expression شنّه ورنّه *shanna wa-ranna*, 'an inquiry and a ringing,' from *šny* ϢⲒⲚⲈ, 'inquiry

شنف *shinf* *ḫnft* ϪⲚⲞϤ, 'basket'

شنودة *Shenūda*, a man's name, *ʿnḫ nṯr* ϢⲈⲚⲞⲨⲦⲈ, 'God lives'

مشوّش *mishawish* ϢⲰϢ, 'confused of mind,' from *š3š3* 'twisted'

شوب *shōb* ϢⲞϨⲂ *šhb*, 'hot weather'

شوبش *shōbash* (later written as) *špst* ϢⲀⲠϢⲒ, 'distinguished, noble women'

شوشة *shūsha*, 'hair,' from *d̲3d̲3* ϪⲒϪⲰⲒ, 'head'

شوطة *shōṭa* *šʿd* ϢⲰⲰⲦ, 'massacre, catastrophe, epidemic'

شونة *shōna* *šnwt* ϢⲈⲨⲚⲈ, 'granary'

شيش *shīsh* *ssd* ϢⲞⲨϢⲦ, 'shuttered windows'

شيكا *shīka* 'finish, take' from *d̲ḳ* (Demotic) ϪⲰⲔ, 'finish,' and *t3w* ϪⲒ, 'take,' found in the expression شيكا بيكا *shīka-bīka!* 'Finish (your work)! Take your salary!'

ص

صير *ṣīr* ϪⲒⲢ, a kind of small fish, eaten with salt and now taken as a metaphor for extremely salty food

ض

ضبّة *ḍabba* *t3 p3yt* ⲦⲈⲠⲰ, part of the fastening of a door

ط

طبّ *ṭabb* *ḥdb* ϨⲦⲞⲠ, 'to fall'

طبطب *ṭabṭab* *t̲bt̲bt*, 'to pat someone's back in gesture of affection'

طرشة *ṭursha*, used in the expression ايد طرشة *īd ṭursha*, 'heavy-handed blows,' from ⲦⲰⲢϢ, perhaps derived from *dšr* 'to be red (with anger?)'

طربش *ṭurubsh*, 'stupid or dull person,' from *tbipsi* (Demotic) ⲦⲈⲢⲠⲞⲤⲈ, 'baked brick'

طوبة *ṭūba* *dbt* ⲦⲰⲂⲈ, 'mud brick'

طوبة *Ṭūba* *t3 ˁb* ⲦⲰⲂⲈ (month)

طورية *ṭūrya* *tr* ⲦⲰⲢⲈ, 'hoe'

طينة (*sakrān*) *ṭīna* *tẖ* ϮϨⲈ or ⲐⲒϧⲒ, 'senselessly (drunk)'

ع

عاد *ˁād*, superfluous particle in a negative sentence, from *ˁn* ⲀⲚ

عبّط *ˁabbaṭ* *ḥpt* ϨⲞⲠⲦ, 'to embrace'

عفّ *ˁaff* *ˁf* ⲀϤ, 'fly'

عفش *ˁifish* *pš3yy* ⲈⲠϢⲈ, 'cockroach or other unpleasant insect'

عك *ˁakk* *3ḳ* ⲀⲔⲰ, 'to destroy'

عيش *ˁaysh* 'life; that which sustains life, bread'; cf. *ˁnẖ*

العيش انقطع *al-ˁaysh inqataˁ*, 'the bread was cut off,' i.e., a job is lost or a relationship is broken

ف

فرعون *firˁūn* *pr ˁ3*, 'pharaoh'

يفرفر *yifarfar* *brbr* ϤⲢϤⲈⲢ, 'to shake, shiver'

فشوش *fashūsh* *p3 ẖ3ẖ3* ⲠϢⲰϢ, 'failure'

يفط *yufuṭṭ* ⲠⲰⲦ, 'to jump,' perhaps from *pd*, 'to run, or run away'

فهلوه *fahlawa* ⲫⲖⲎⲞⲨ or ⲈⲠⲢⲀ, 'deceit,' perhaps from *prt* 'vanities'

فوطة *fūṭa* *fty* ϥⲱⲧⲉ, 'towel'

فول *fūl* *pr* ⲫⲉⲗ, 'fava beans'

ق

قرص *qurṣ,* a round baked or fried cake, from ⲕⲣⲟⲩϫ, 'a disk, something round'

قَرْموط *qarmūṭ,* 'catfish,' euphemism for phallus

قلتة *Qulta,* a man's name, from or *krṯ* ⲕⲉⲗⲗⲟϫ 'puppy'

ك

ياكاسي *ya kāsi,* 'oh my burial!' from *ḳrst* ⲕⲁⲓⲥⲉ, 'burial'

كاكولة *kakūla,* 'long overcoat,' from ⲕⲟⲩⲕⲗⲁ from Greek κουκούλλιον, 'a hood or cowl of monks'

كاني *kānī,* used in the expression كاني وماني *kānī wa-mānī* to express harmony, from *ḳny* ⲕⲏⲛⲉ, 'fat'

كبّب *kabbib,* 'to accumulate,' from *ḳ3b* ⲕⲱⲃ 'doubling'

كلكوعة *kalkūʿa* ⲕⲉⲗⲕⲟⲩⲗⲉ or ⲕⲗⲕⲁ, 'a lump,' perhaps related to *k3k3wt*

كرتة *karta* *ḳrṯt* (Demotic) ⲕⲉⲣⲏⲧ, 'remains of a meal'

كنافة *kunāfa,* a kind of Egyptian sweet pastry, possibly from *ẖnfw* ⲕⲉⲛⲉⲫⲓⲧⲉⲛ

كعك *kaʿk* *kʿk* ⲕⲁⲁⲕⲉ, an Egyptian cookie

كيهك *Kiyahk* *k3 ḥr k3* ⲕⲟⲓⲁϩⲕ (month)

ل

لبيس *labīs lbs* (Demotic) ⲖⲞⲂⲤ, a kind of Nile fish

متلقح *mitlaqqaḥ,* 'neglected,' from *rḳꜥ* ⲖⲀⲔϨ, 'corner'

لفت *lift* ⲖⲀⲠⲦ or ⲖⲀⲦⲠ, 'salt turnip, pickled turnip'

لكش *lakash* *nsḳ* ⲖⲰⲔⲤ, 'to attack'

ياليل *ya lēl*, traditional introduction to many Egyptian songs, from ⲖⲞⲨⲖⲀⲒ, 'to shout (with joy)'

م

ما *ma*, a particle sometimes prefixed to a verb to make an imperative, as in the expression ماتشتغل *ma-tishtaghal!* 'get to work!' from ⲘⲀⲢⲈ, 'let (us go)'

مجور *majūr* ⲘⲀⲔⲢⲞ, 'a type of mortar,' perhaps related to *mḳr*, 'vessel'

مريسي *marīsi* 'south wind,' from *rsy* ⲢⲎⲤ

مريسة *marīsa* *mrsw* ⲘⲢⲒⲤ, a kind of Egyptian beer

مسرى *Misra* *msw rꜥ* ⲘⲈⲤⲰⲢⲎ (month)

مش *mish* *bw rẖ* ⲘⲈϢⲈ, 'not'

مصطبة *maṣṭaba,* a crude brick seat, from *mstpt*, 'box'

مم *mam*, food, *my wnm*, 'give to eat,' ⲘⲀⲨⲰⲘ

ميت *mīt* ⲘⲞⲈⲒⲦ, 'way,' used in compound place names, such as *Mīt Ghamr* and *Mīt Abu al-Kōm*

ن

ناف *nāf* *nḥb.f* ⲚⲀϨⲂⲈϤ, 'yoke'

ناني *nāni,* 'honeycomb,' from *mnỉ* ⲚⲎⲚⲒ, 'honey pot'

نبأ *naba'* *nb* ⲚⲞⲨⲂ, 'gold'

نباري *nabāri* *npry* ⲚⲀⲠⲢⲈ, 'grain'

نبوت *nabbūt* *nbỉt*, 'rod'

نف *naff* *nf* ⲚⲒϤⲒ, ' to blow one's nose'

نفرت *Nufret*, an ancient woman's name revived for modern use, from *nfrt*, 'the beautiful one'

نفرتاري *Nefertari*, an ancient woman's name revived for modern use, from *nfrt.iry*, 'their beautiful one'

نفرتيتي *Nefertiti*, an ancient woman's name revived for modern use, from *nfrt ỉtỉ*, 'the beautiful one has come'

ننوس *nannūs*, *nꜣ ʿn.s* ⲚⲀⲚⲞⲨⲤ, 'she is beautiful' (a pet name)

نوب *nūb* *nb* ⲚⲞⲨⲂ, 'gold,' used in the expression هوب هوب ياشغل النوب *hōb, hōb, ya shughl al-nōb,* 'Work, work! Work is gold!'

نوري *nūri,* 'a rapacious imposter,' from *nrt* ⲚⲞⲨⲢⲈ, 'vulture'

نونو *nūnu* *nnỉ* ⲚⲞⲨⲚⲈ(ⲞⲨ), 'child or infant'

ه

هاتور *Hatūr* *ḥt ḥr* ϨⲀⲦⲰⲢ (month)

هرّ *harr*, 'to have diarrhea,' from *ḥry* ϨⲞⲒⲢⲈ, 'dung'

هروة *hiriwwa* *ẖrt* ϩⲣⲉⲩⲉ, 'food'

مهلهل *mihalhil* ϩⲟⲗϩⲗ, 'in tatters,' perhaps from *ẖnẖn*, 'to scatter'

هنّن *hannin* *hnhn* ϩⲗⲟⲟⲗⲉ, 'to lull'

هوب *hūb* *h3b* ϩⲱⲃ, 'work,' used in the expression هوب هوب ياشغل النوب *hōb, hōb, ya shughl al-nōb,* 'Work, work! Work is gold!'

هوسة *hawsa* *ḥsy* ϩⲱⲥ, 'to sing'

هيصة *hēṣa* *ẖzy* ϩⲓⲥⲉ, 'trouble'

و

يوحوح *yiwaḥwaḥ* *wḥwḥ* ⲟⲩⲁϩⲃⲉϥ, 'to groan'

وحوي ياوحوي ايوحة *waḥawy ya waḥawy iyūḥa* 'welcome, welcome, o crescent,' from Coptic expression ⲟⲩⲱϩ ⲟⲩⲱϩ ⲓⲟϩ, derived from *w3ḥ*, 'to stay, put,' and *iʿḥ,* 'moon'

ويبة *wēba* *ỉp.t* ⲟⲓⲡⲉ, a unit of measurement of dry weight

ي

يم *yamm* *ym* ⲓⲟⲙ, 'sea'

Sources

ANET = *Ancient Near Eastern Texts* (Pritchard)
Tale of Sinuhe = *The Tale of Sinuhe* (in Parkinson)
URK = *Urkunden des ägyptischen Altertums* (Steindorff)
Wb = *Wörterbuch der aegyptischen Sprache* (Erman)
ZÄS = *Zeitschrift für ägyptische Sprache und Altertumskunde*

Crum, W.E. *A Coptic Dictionary*. Oxford: Clarendon Press, 1990, c1939.

Černy, J. *Coptic Etymological Dictionary*. New York: Cambridge University Press, 1976.

Erman, Adolf and Hermann Grapow. *Wörterbuch der aegyptischen Sprache*. Berlin: Academie Verlag, [reprint] 1971.

Gardiner, Alan. *Egyptian Grammar*. Third Edition, revised. Oxford: Ashmolean Museum, 1976.

Herodotus. *The History* (translated by David Greene). Chicago: University of Chicago Press, 1987.

Hinds, Martin, and el-Said Badawi. *A Dictionary of Egyptian Arabic: Arabic–English*. Beirut: Librairie du Liban, 1986.

Lambdin, Thomas O. *Introduction to Sahidic Coptic.* Macon, Ga.: Mercer University Press, 1983.

Parkinson, R.B. *The Tale of Sinuhe and Other Ancient Egyptian Poems, 1940–1640 BC.* Oxford University Press, 1997.

Pritchard, James B. *Ancient Near Eastern Texts Relating to the Old Testament.* Princeton University Press, 1969 (third edition).

Sobhy, Georgy. *Common Words in the Spoken Arabic of Egypt of Greek or Coptic Origin*. Cairo: La Société Archéologie Copte, 1950.

Spiro, Socrates. *An Arabic–English Dictionary of the Colloquial Arabic of Egypt.* Beirut: Librairie du Liban, 1973.

Steindorff, Georg. *Urkunden des ägyptischen Altertums.* Leipzig: Hinrichs, 1903–.

Vycichl, Werner. *Dictionnaire etymologique de la langue Copte.* Leuven: Peeters, 1983.